table of contents

I. Mindset + Stress Management 14

   DAYS 1 - 5

II. Cleansing 41

   DAYS 6 - 12

III. Movement 74

   DAY 13

IV. Nutrition 78

   DAY 14

V. Connection 84

   DAYS 15 - 18

VI. Manifesting 97

   DAYS 19 - 21

Hi Love,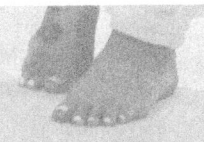

We are so excited to be connecting for this transformative Elevate Higher 21-day challenge with you! We couldn't be happier that you are here with us and ready to take your life to new levels and make your dreams a reality.

If this is our first meeting, we are Britt + Tara - high-vibrational living experts, Kundalini yoga and meditation instructors, creators of Elevate the Globe and two best friends on a mission to do our part to leave the world better than when we came here. Whether you've been a part of our tribe for some time now or you're brand new to ETG, we know you will love this experience!

We encourage you to connect with us online during this challenge, both in our Facebook group (The Elevate The Globe Spiritual Warriors) and over on Instagram (@elevatetheglobe) using and following the hashtag #elevatehigherchallenge. To get the Elevate Higher Toolkit bonus resources for this challenge make sure to put your email and amazon order number in over at www.elevatetheglobe.com/21dayelevatehigherchallenge! It is so great to connect with the community as you are doing this work. By sharing when you feel called to, we can all learn from and help each other rise higher together.

We are here for you as your guides and will be cheering you on the whole way through. We will be going live on Facebook and Instagram and will have the live recordings available for you to watch everyday to get more inspiration and insight. No matter when you are embarking on this challenge with us you can access the 21-Day Challenge Tool Kit at elevatetheglobe.com/21dayelevatehighertoolkit to get the replays and all the resources referenced in the workbook.

We are giving you an energetic high five for committing to yourself and your life in a more significant way. All you have to do is follow along and complete the daily challenges, and everything else will take care of itself.

If it ever feels hard to keep up, just take one baby step and know that "when you keep up, you will be kept up!" as Yogi Bhajan said. Trust in the process and know that you deserve everything that is coming and everything is happening just as it should. Enjoy this journey!

A little more about us before we get started ...

Meet Britt!

I'm Britt, co-founder of Elevate the Globe, certified IKYTA Kundalini yoga teacher, spiritual leader, mama + wife — and I just think of myself as a happy and grateful human. While growing up, I always had an obsession with self-help books. After my parents divorced, I had a passion for deepening my understanding of life and my higher self, and for seeking the truth in my life's purpose and close relationships. In high school and college, I began to feel inspired to pursue my ability to manifest with the Law of Attraction. However, it wasn't until after college, when my life took a hectic turn, that I truly realized the magic of living a high vibrational life.

After college, I felt alone and lost. I started partying hard, using Hollywood nightlife, alcohol, and drugs to numb my pain while avoiding the challenges of heartbreak after breaking up with my boyfriend. Although I was doing very well in my corporate career in advertising sales, I started to notice how my big commission checks were not giving me the happiness I thought they would. I knew there was something more to life and was determined to find it.

As the universe would have it, one day I stumbled into a Kundalini yoga class at Equinox in West Hollywood and my transformation began. Although I had no clue what I was doing - I was only there to work out my abs - I felt completely connected to myself and experienced a moment of clarity in class. I continued taking that same class every week and began to notice a massive shift in my mood, thoughts, and energy. The more I practiced, the more I began to realize how my state of mind was directly related to the positivity surrounding me, gaining a sense of peace and happiness while improving my overall health.

These positive changes led me to fully commit to my practice, and I transitioned to living a healthy lifestyle. I started practicing yoga and meditation consistently. I said goodbye to drugs and binge drinking and gave the warmest "hello" to clean, high-vibe living, and everything began to change for the better. I went to Costa Rica on a Kundalini yoga retreat and then dedicated 9 months to train and become a Kundalini yoga instructor in 2013 under Guru Singh at Yoga West in LA.

In 2015, about a year after my wedding, my mother passed after an 11-month battle with lung cancer. Although this loss was the hardest thing I have ever experienced, losing my mom has given me a greater appreciation for life and has strengthened my commitment to sharing my passion for health and wellness with others. Without my healthy practices, I would not have been able to cope with her loss as well as I have been able to. My primary goal is to appreciate every day while leaving something behind that would make the world a little better. It was from this goal and passion that Elevate the Globe was born with co-founder and childhood friend Tara Schulenberg.

I currently reside in LA with my husband, Justin, daughter, Everest, and yellow lab, Iris.

Meet Tara!

I'm Tara, co-founder of Elevate the Globe, a high-vibrational wellness coach, IKYTA Kundalini yoga teacher and astrology practitioner. As a teenager, I was always drawn to astrology and numerology - signs, meanings, birthdays, and connecting the dots always seemed to fascinate me. Fast forward to 2012: After a four-year relationship ended in a painful breakup, I was floundering, seeing a psychiatrist, taking medication to numb my pain, excessively dating different men, and generally searching for some clarity, understanding, and life answers. Emotionally, I was a wreck and hiding my emotions and negative habits from family and friends. After some soul searching, I turned back to my passion for astrology as a way to understand the entire chain of my life's events. I began connecting with psychics for guidance and learned how to properly tune in, listen to my intuition, and activate my own clairvoyant abilities.

The real transformation started when I began taking Kundalini yoga classes in San Francisco, after hearing about it from my childhood best friend, Britt. I spent my Sundays on my mat practicing Kundalini at the Guru Ram Das Ashram in the Haight, and it became my weekly ritual. I'd take a class, sit and have coffee at the cafe down the street by myself, and shop for crystals. It was magical, and everything started to change...and quickly. My attitude was all about having fun and being open to new experiences, and those are the exact things I began to attract into my life.

Three months into my Kundalini practice, I had the most clarity on life I had ever experienced. It happened to be on the weekend Britt's mom passed away. I could hear Britt's mom's voice very clearly in my ear that it was time to move home, back to Los Angeles. I needed to be with Britt, and I needed to be with my own mom. A couple months later, I made the move to LA and went deep into my Kundalini practice.

I could sense there was a profound career plan trying to make itself known to me, but I could not connect to the message until Britt and I were guided to see the Brazilian healer John of God. It was there in New York, where we both received a two-hour download from the universe, that I could visually see our soul mission unfolding in front of me. It was the most incredible and esoteric experience, and it's how Elevate the Globe began.

I currently reside in LA with my angel of a dog, Rex.

Welcome to the first day of the rest of your life!

We're BEYOND thrilled you're embarking on this journey with us. This is an exciting new chapter for you that's bursting with possibilities, surprises, and the unknown...

Dun dun dun! We know, the unknown may feel a bit scary to you at times. On the flip side, it's super exciting because anything is possible. The universe is limitless, you are limitless, and magic and miracles are real. If you don't believe in them yet, you just haven't experienced them thus far - but, we assure you, you want to. (And you can!)

Our intention with this challenge is to give you tools and inspiration to open yourself up, break down any walls, blocks, or limitations, and bring more energy into your body, mind, and aura. When you do that, you can access the higher-vibration emotions like love, joy, and freedom. From those higher frequencies, it'll be easier to attract the things you want. In this elevated place, you'll feel good, and you'll have your needs met, so it'll be natural to want to give back to others and to the planet. And when you're doing good in the world, you can manifest even more. The opportunities that were always available to you will start to become clear — and they'll show up fast.

"Vibration, frequencies ... what the hell are you guys talking about?"

If that's what you're thinking right now, don't stress. The thing is, *everything* is energy. Once you understand that scientific fact, everything we're about to teach you will make sense. We're gonna break it down a little more so your brain can fully get behind this adventure, but just know that everything you need to understand will be unlocked in perfect timing.

To start, quite simply, raising your vibration is all about physics. According to Einstein's relativity equation — $E=MC^2$ — 99.99% of everything is energy vibrating at a specific frequency. Yup, even the chair you're sitting on and this workbook you're reading. That can be a confusing concept when the world around you appears to be solid, but it's really just mass that's made up of an F-ton of moving energy.

The Law of Vibration

The Law of Vibration — one of the 12 Universal Laws that metaphysical scholars laid out 5,000 years ago — also states that everything is made of energy, which means we as humans are all made up of energy. But this law goes a step beyond what you may have learned in high-school science class: It states that our energy is vibrating at a frequency that is attracting everything in our lives, whether we are aware of it, understand it, or not.

So how do you know where your energetic vibration is at any given time? It's easy — you just need to check in with your emotions, which each have a vibratory frequency of their own. We love to reference the Abraham-Hicks Emotional Guidance Scale because it shows us the exact frequency in Hz of every emotion we experience. The Emotional Scale is like an energetic roadmap. You can use it to figure out where you are now and guide yourself to where you want to be.

As you can see in the image on the next page, higher-frequency emotions equal higher-frequency energy. So when we say "raise your vibration", we're really talking about moving into an elevated emotional state.

But if you've ever been stuck in a place of frustration, worry, or anger, you'll know that it's not always simple to just choose optimism, enthusiasm, or joy instead. In fact, it can sometimes feel straight-up impossible.

ELEVATE**THE**GLOBE

The Emotional Guidance Scale

Brainwave Frequency

- 600- 900+ Hz
- 500+ Hz
- 400+ Hz
- 300+ Hz
- 250 Hz
- 200+ Hz
- 175+ Hz
- 150+ Hz
- 125+ Hz
- 50 Hz
- 20 Hz
- 0 DEATH

1. Joy/Appreciation/Empowered/Freedom
2. Love
3. Passion
4. Enthusiasm/Eagerness/Happiness
5. Positive Expectation/Belief
6. Optimism
7. Hopefulness
8. Contentment
9. Boredom
10. Pessimism
11. Frustration/Irritation/Impatience
12. Overwhelment
13. Disappointment
14. Doubt
15. Worry
16. Blame
17. Discouragement
18. Anger
19. Revenge
20. Hatred/Rage
21. Jealousy
22. Insecurity/Guilt/Unworthiness
23. Fear/Grief/Depression/Despair/Powerlessness

Here's why:

To move into the higher-frequency emotions, our nervous systems must have the ability to run those frequencies through our bodies. And if we want to hold on to those high-vibe emotions, our nervous systems need to be able to handle high frequencies for long periods. This is why we focus so much on Kundalini yoga at Elevate the Globe, and why we'll be doing a lot of it in this challenge. It's a technology that clears out the subconscious mind and the energy blockages in the body so energy can flow through us with ease. We become a clearer channel and vessel for the light to come through us.

There are a few things we want to make sure you understand about emotions before we start to practice tools and techniques to move up the Emotional Scale. (Don't worry, we'll get there soon!)

1. Our unconscious thoughts play a significant role in how we feel.

Our emotional state is influenced by ideas formed and held in the subconscious mind, where we're not even aware of them. We as humans tend to suppress emotions, and these suppressed emotions may lead to depression, anxiety, and other challenges when they are not healed and released. It's like we're holding on to mounds of emotional weight in our subconscious minds and don't even realize it.

2. We all feel the entire spectrum of emotions on the emotional scale.

No matter how high-vibe you are, you will still feel the lower emotions sometimes. You don't need to feel bad or guilty about having them, but just accept where you are and then use the tools in this challenge to heal, feel better and move up the scale...on the daily. You'll start to feel certain emotions more often, and you'll want to hang out with people who are on the same frequency (emotional state) as you. (Insert law of attraction...but more on that later.)

3. Feelings are contagious: Your own and others'.

Good feelings lead to more good feelings, and negative feelings lead to feeling worse. This explains the spiral or the arrows on the Emotional Scale. From contentment and up, you are on the upward spiral. Boredom and down are on the downward spiral. Womp womp.

Okay, so we're pretty sure your physics teachers didn't show you how your vibration can help you get through that breakup, lose weight, find love, go for your dreams ... and, most importantly, to just seriously feel fucking better while you go through your daily routine. But that's why you've got us!

Getting Over Commitment-Phobia

We'll discuss the Emotional Scale in more detail soon, but for now, we want to set you up for success. Why? Because we've set ourselves up for failure one too many times, and you might have also. But doing things differently is what this challenge is all about, and we want to guide you to choose a different flavor than you usually do.

We've created a few pre-challenge exercises to help you fully commit to the next 21 days. Our subconscious minds like to pull from the past and replicate it so this exercise will help us break that cycle and create a new pattern!

PRE-CHALLENGE PROMPT #1

If you've ever started something and not finished it, write it out here:

_____

_____

_____

_____

_____

_____

_____

_____

Now, for each one of the things you've written down, say to yourself "I forgive you, you did the best you could."

Depending on how many things you wrote, you'll start to realize how committed (ex: You have 1-2 things listed) or non-committal (ex: You have 10+ things listed) you've been in the past.

But — and this is key — don't get down on yourself if you've had a hard time committing to things before! That's where the forgiveness comes in. Once you're aware of that story, you can shift it. Just because you did something a certain way before, that doesn't mean it has to be your reality moving forward.

We can decide to rewrite our story and reshape our reality at any given moment. We just have to give ourselves permission to change and decide to commit to our own evolution. If you're having trouble with commitment, know that we were totally there, too. And if we can change, so can you!

Let's start by committing to this challenge for the next 21 days.

Commitment is the first step to happiness. If you can't commit, then what the F is the point of anything? If you don't commit to anything, you're not giving yourself a chance to grow and see what is actually possible! We need you to commit fully to this challenge ... because it really is important.

Why? Because the planet needs us now. From school shootings to high disease rates to global warming, it's clear there's a lot of healing work that must be done for humanity and the environment. Mother Earth wants us to live at a higher frequency for ourselves and the planet.

We need more people putting time and energy into their mental health. We need more people who are being an example of change and a part of the solution. We need more people who are healthy, happy, and conscious teaching the next generations how to feel good and live well. We need less pain and suffering as a society to truly elevate from where we are to a better life and future for us all.

We bring this up not to focus on the negative, but to be aware of why it's a crucial time for us all to be emissaries of light and positive vibrations. And you can do your part towards healing these big planetary issues by starting with you! As you raise your vibration, it'll have a ripple effect on your family, your friends, and your community.

If you need some extra commitment inspo, check out Episode 38 of our podcast, The Elevator — "Commitment: Why it's SO Important".

Remember the Emotional Scale? When more people raise their vibration, there will be less fear, anger, sadness, shame, and guilt feeding into the way everyone operates on this planet because fewer people will be in those lower vibrations. Instead, there will be more love, forgiveness, freedom, joy, and enlightenment. And in a world with more of that energy, a lot of good can happen. We believe in you!

"Be the change you wish to see in the world." - Mahatma Gandhi

PRE-CHALLENGE PROMPT #2

Write down why you are committing. Being aware of your WHY is so important because it's your inspiration for sticking with this commitment — and you can come back to that inspiration if things start to feel hard.

_____

_____

_____

_____

_____

PRE-CHALLENGE PROMPT #3

Write a little bit about how you're feeling now and any challenge or struggle you feel. What's your biggest pain point or area you are ready to heal? This will help you reflect back and compare how you feel at the end of the challenge.

_____

_____

_____

_____

_____

Pro Tip- Write it out on another piece of paper or take a picture of your "why" statement and put it somewhere you can see it every day! Feel free to also post it on Instagram Stories and tag us (@elevatetheglobe) or in our Facebook group, **The Elevate the Globe Spiritual Warriors**, if you want more accountability. (You'll also inspire others to do the same!) Having support is key to success. So we encourage you to connect with others and share your experience as much as possible.

How To Stay Committed ...
When You Really Don't Want To

You're all in! No backing out now, LOL. But don't worry, we're here with you the whole time.

Here are some **other tips** to help you keep up with your commitment to the 21-day challenge:

1. **Create a time and place to connect with this work every day. Maybe it's in the bathroom before your shower or next to your bed — just find somewhere that works best for you to get it done each day.**

2. **Set an alarm on your phone to remind yourself to check in on where you're at with the challenge.**

3. **Do it with a friend! Feel free to invite anyone you know to be your accountability buddy, or pair up with someone in our Facebook group, The Elevate the Globe Spiritual Warriors.**

4. **Meditate throughout the challenge. Meditating will help keep you present and connected to your WHY. It will give you more energy and will allow you to hold the higher-frequency emotions that will keep you moving forward with this challenge and your life.**

Now, you're ready to understand how this all works on a deeper level. You're ready to start living differently — living better — and that's why you're here.

Whether you've been studying energy for years or this is your first raising-your-vibration rodeo, there is always growth and expansion available for you. It's just up to you how much you will allow. This workbook is in your hands because it's exactly what you need right now, in this very moment. It was channeled through us because it's necessary for more humans to be engaging in this work, elevating their energetic vibration, and we're so happy it has made its way to you. Virtual high fives for being here and for showing up!

xoxo SAT NAM, **B + T**

DAY 1: Get Clear On Your Intentions

Okay, who's ready?!! Let's get started on this magical adventure! The first step of manifesting anything is getting clear on what you want. Since we are manifesting higher vibrations here, we have to get clear about what that looks like. You don't need to have all the answers — we sure don't — but you do need to have a specific intention of what you want to bring to your life and how you want to feel.

If you don't have a vision of where you want to go, you could end up anywhere. Think of it this way: If you wanted to go to Hawaii, you would choose an island, buy a plane ticket, book a hotel, that kind of thing. But not getting clear is like going to the airport and just blindly hopping on any plane without knowing where you're going. Sure, the final destination might be okay, but it probably wouldn't match the vision of your vacation that you had in your head. You may not have packed correctly, you might not be sipping a pineapple smoothie by the pool — and you'd probably be a little disappointed.

That's how energy and manifesting works. When you have clarity and direction, your mind will align with your desire, and you'll feel inspired to take action towards your goal. You'll get to where you want to go, where your soul is calling and where your destiny lies. It's that simple.

So how to get clear? We meditate!

A lot of times we don't know what we want because our mind is too cluttered. The untrained mind is like a monkey jumping all over the place. (That's why you hear it called the "monkey mind.") If your subconscious mind is clogged up with past memories, traumas, thoughts, and fears, it'll be hard to be present enough to get clear on your desires. Plus, it's our subconscious minds that drive our point of attraction and our actions — not our conscious thoughts. This is one of the many reasons why having a daily meditation practice is so important in general, and especially for this challenge. We need to clear our subconscious of all the hidden blocks piled up inside our brains.

Meditation releases all the junk from our subconscious and conscious mind — the stuff that isn't serving the highest good of our soul and the planet. And if that's not enough to convince you, there are tons of other mental and physical benefits of meditation. We could fill a whole book with them: It reduces stress, improves sleep, increases our focus, improves relationships, boosts the immune and nervous systems, and more.

"Before I really had clarity I was manifesting a lot but my manifestations were all over the place and would show up in weird ways — not exactly how I wanted and not exactly better. It was when I got clear through meditation and journaling with the prompts below that I really started creating the life of my dreams." - **Britt**

TODAY'S CHALLENGE

If you've never meditated before, just know you can start small. Even three minutes of meditation can make a major impact. Today's task is to do just that — here's how it's done.

Let's release stress and duality for positive energy with this meditation. The goal is to practice this one every day for the challenge or as much as you can!!

The five elements, or tattvas, are Earth, Water, Fire, Air and Ether. If the tattvas are strong, in balance, and located in their proper areas of the body, then you can resist stress, trauma, and illness.

Yogis have long recognized that the best decision-making takes place when the left and right hemispheres of the brain are balanced and synchronized. Since the left brain questions and the right brain accepts, an individual's analytical and creative thought processes are most effective when a state of balance in neutrality is achieved.

Step 1 Tune in with the Adi Mantra Ong Namo Guru Dev Namo:

This is how we tune in before doing any Kundalini Yoga or meditation and it just means I bow to the divine wisdom within and connects you to yourself and the lineage of yogis that came before us. You can catch the video of how to tune in over at https://elevatetheglobe.com/21dayelevatehighertoolkit!

Step 2 Posture*:
Sit in Easy Pose with a straight spine. Raise the arms with the elbows bent until the hands meet at the level of the heart in front of the chest. The forearms make a straight line parallel to the ground.

Step 3 Mudra: Spread the fingers of both hands. Touch the fingertips and thumb tips of opposite hands together. Create enough pressure to join the first segments (counting from the tip) of each finger. The thumbs are stretched back and point toward the torso. The fingers are bent slightly due to the pressure. The palms are separated.

Step 4 Eyes: Fix your eyes at the tip of the nose.

Step 5 Breath: Inhale slowly and deeply through the nose. Exhale through the rounded lips in eight equal, emphatic strokes. On each exhale, pull the navel point in sharply. Continue for 3 minutes. You may build the practice slowly to 11 minutes but note that longer times are only for the dedicated, serious practitioners.

Step 6 To End: Then inhale deeply, hold for 10-30 seconds, and exhale. Inhale again, and shake the hands over the head. Relax.

Benefits according to Yogi Bhajan: If the five elements (tattvas) are strong, in balance, and located in their proper areas of the body, then you can resist stress, trauma, and illness. You do not get confused in conflicts between the two hemispheres of the brain as they compete for the right to make and direct decisions.

This meditation uses the hand mudra to pressure the 10 radiance points in the fingers that correlate to the zones of the brain in the two hemispheres. The equal pressure causes a kind of communication and coordination between the two hemispheres of the brain.

The deep inhale gives endurance and calmness. The exhale through the mouth strengthens the parasympathetic system from a control band of reflexes in the ring of the throat. This calms reactions to stress.

The strokes of the exhale stimulate the pituitary to optimize your clarity, intuition, and decision-making capacities. It resolves many inner conflicts, especially when the conflicts are from different levels of your functioning: spiritual versus mental versus physical or survival needs.

BONUS: Go over to www.elevatetheglobe.com/21dayelevatehighertoolkit and press play to practice a meditation video with us. Feel free to take a picture of yourself or your meditation set up and tag us @elevatetheglobe on Insta or post in the FB group to inspire more people to get on their mat!!

*If you're a member of our 528 Academy or RISE UP, feel free to choose a meditation from those programs — or any other meditation you feel called to — for the meditation piece.

After your meditation today, ask the universe to help you get clear on what you want and deliver anything you need to hear. Take as much time as you need to sit in silence and listen. Then, answer today's journal prompts:

Why is it important for you to heal and release any low-vibration emotions out of your life?

_____
_____
_____
_____
_____
_____
_____
_____

What are you ready to leave behind?

_____
_____
_____

What are you ready to bring in?

How do you want to feel at the end of this challenge?

_____
_____
_____
_____
_____
_____
_____
_____

What are three specific things you want to manifest now?
Write them in present tense.

(Ex: "I am so happy and grateful I am pregnant. I am so happy and grateful I am the proud owner of a new Tesla. I am so happy and grateful I found my dream partner. I am so happy and grateful I healed myself of Lyme disease and am moving towards optimal health every day.")

_____
_____
_____

Read your manifestations out loud, and end by saying:

"AND SO IT IS!"

DAY 2: Get To Know Your Low-Vibe Thoughts

We introduced you to the Emotional Scale a couple days ago, and now we're going to take a closer look at the principles behind it. Isn't it liberating to realize that all of the human emotions are measured in energy, and all of us have the ability to move into a higher-vibration emotion? When you think of it like that everything seems possible, right?

Everything is energy.

First, let's dive a little deeper into the science of energy work. As we mentioned before, Einstein's $E=MC^2$ discovery proved everything is energy, even matter that may appear to be solid. When you look through a high-powered microscope, you begin to see substances broken down into their smallest components — atoms vibrating at different frequencies. Quantum physics shows us matter is ultimately empty space interspersed with energy. Our bodies are no exception.

Your energetic vibration creates your reality.

Now let's move to the Law of Vibration. This universal law also states that anything that exists in our universe, seen or unseen — when broken down and analyzed in its purest and most basic form — consists of pure energy or light. And all of this energy is vibrating at certain speeds, on different frequencies.

The Law of Vibration also states that all things, thoughts, feelings, and actions attract things of the same vibrational frequency. In other words, your emotional vibration affects everything around you and helps shape your life as you know it. Your environment, people, animals, objects, situations — all of it!

Plus, since everything in the universe is connected, vibrationally speaking, your emotions also affect other people and the planet. Our energy is contributing to the big bowl of energy that makes up the universe. It's kind of like when you're making a recipe, how the taste and quality of each ingredient will affect the way the final meal tastes. That's how it works with our energy, and how it contributes to the overall energy of the planet.

Chances are you know someone who feels really good to be around. You can probably also think of someone who makes you uneasy, but you can't really explain why. In both of these cases, you're picking up on their high and low vibrations, respectively. The truth is, we all bring energy into every situation, and we're each responsible for the energy we contribute to the planet. Like we said before, we never want you to feel anxious or guilty if you're having a low-vibe day. But we can all be aware of what we can do to heal and bring better energy to the planet.

Your vibration begins with your thoughts.

One more universal law we have to share with you to drive this concept home is the Law of Mentalism.

The Law of Mentalism

"Everything is mental; the Universe is a mental creation of the All." This basically means everything begins in the mind.

When your mind habitually thinks thoughts of a certain quality, the Law of Mentalism explains that these thoughts embed into your subconscious mind and become your main emotional vibration. This vibration resonates with similar vibrations and attracts them into your life. So if you think about getting fired from your job every day, it creates an emotional vibration of fear. And according to the Law of Mentalism, this fearful vibration will draw the things you fear into your life. The good news? The same thing is said to happen with positive thoughts and positive experiences.

Elevate your thoughts, elevate your life.

So how do we create a reality we actually want? The first step is we want to become super aware of our conscious thoughts and the resulting emotions so we can start to flip the script. We can heal any limiting beliefs or ideas binding us to lower consciousness by looking at them, moving the energy, and sending new information into our subconscious. And one great way to do this is through Kundalini yoga and meditation, AKA the "yoga of awareness". Throughout this challenge we'll be practicing this form of yoga, which helps us recognize our conscious thoughts and clears out the subconscious mind.

"Meditation is to become aware of every thought and of every feeling, never to say it is right or wrong, but just to watch it and move with it. In that watching, you begin to understand the whole movement of thought and feeling. And out of this awareness becomes silence." - *Jiddu Krishnamurti*

TODAY'S CHALLENGE

Print out the Emotional Scale and/or save it on your phone. Keep it somewhere you can see it, like by your bedside or on your bathroom mirror. Then, complete today's journal prompts:

Identify where you are on the emotional scale most days and list the thoughts that come with these emotions.

_____

_____

_____

_____

_____

_____

_____

_____

Next, identify where you want to be and why.

_____

_____

_____

_____

_____

_____

_____

_____

_____

_____

_____

_____

Get into the energy of checking in with the scale throughout the day and every day — whenever you feel called — and start to make this a practice in your life. Becoming aware of where you are now is the first step. You're doing great!

Today's mantra and one to use throughout the rest of the challenge:

"It is my dominant intent to feel good" - Abraham Hicks

DAY 3: Breathe Like A Yogi

Amazing job! You are starting to do the conscious work of becoming more aware of your thoughts and feelings. The thing is, this requires you to be present throughout the day, which isn't always easy when you've got a packed to-do list and a constantly dinging phone. So today we're going to focus on the number-one tool we use to stay present: THE BREATH!

Were you ever taught how to breathe? Do you ever think about breathing? Probably not — breathing is an involuntary thing. But it's incredibly important, as it gives you life. And it determines your quality of life more than you may realize. As any yoga or meditation instructor will tell you, connecting to your breath is also the fastest, easiest way to become more mindful. Your breath is with you through every moment of every day, and it's something you can control. (We all know that's not the case for many aspects of life).

"Realize deeply that the present moment is all you ever have." — Eckhart Tolle

Breathe your way to peace.

Mindfulness is the basic human ability to be fully present. The power of being present is living and feeling the current moment, without dwelling on the past or fretting about the future. When we reflect back to yesterday and how our thoughts affect our emotions, mindfulness helps us stay centered and grounded, as opposed to being overly reactive or overwhelmed by what's going on around us. It gives us the ability to see our thoughts and choose which ones we want to project, put energy behind, and manifest into our realities.

We can start to practice mindfulness by consciously breathing more slowly and deeply. There are so many things in life we practice to get good at — riding a bike, painting, or playing an instrument. But what about fucking breathing, living in the now, and living well? Excuse our FRENCH, but think about that for a minute! LOL!

Breathing correctly and consciously also improves the functioning of our organs, systems (nervous, immune, glandular and lymph) and the brain and sends more oxygen to all of our cells, allowing energy to flow freely throughout the body. It promotes overall better health, vitality, and higher consciousness.

It also helps you to become more abundant. Yep, really! That's because when you breathe in more life-force energy on the daily, you, therefore, have more energy available to you. This means you can hold those higher emotional frequencies longer, which attract more abundance and prosperity to you!

So, for many reasons, it's time to go back to the basics and create a strong foundation of breath we can build upon — one that will last a lifetime. If this freaks you out or makes you uncomfortable, it's totally okay. Take a moment to celebrate that feeling. You're doing the work, and it's not always going to be easy. But navigating discomfort is what will allow you to raise your consciousness, your vibration, and get you feeling how you want to feel.

"I used to play small a lot because I didn't have enough energy to manifest and take action to go bigger in my life. It was when I started using the breath and understanding that the breath is LIFE FORCE ENERGY, that I was able to use breathwork to gain more energy and go bigger in so many areas. Ultimately, breath work put me in the frequency to come together with Britt to create Elevate the Globe — and it also helped me heal and feel better in so many ways. It's all about the breath!" - **Tara**

"In any given moment we have two options: to step forward into growth or step back into safety" - *Abraham Maslow*

TODAY'S CHALLENGE

First, we want you to start paying attention to your breathing patterns. Once you have that awareness, you can work on breathing in a way that promotes higher-vibrational thoughts and emotions. You're going to time your breath and then work to slow it down.

Here's how:

Step 1: Sit or stand and set a timer for one minute.

Step 2: Don't try to control your breath — just breathe naturally and count your breaths (count one for each inhale-exhale combo).

Step 3: Check your results and record them below:
- Over 25 Breaths: Stressed Out
- 20-25 Breaths: Average
- 10 Breaths: Good Health
- 7-9 Breaths: Mentally Balanced
- 0-7 Breaths: Yogi

Date: _____

Breaths Per Minute: _____

Feel free to come back throughout the challenge and test your breath again — it's fun to watch yourself improve!

"When you consciously control your breathing rate, you can control your state of mind." - Yogi Bhajan

Next, let's work on connecting with our breath. Practice breathing slower whenever you can — it's beneficial for all sorts of reasons, according to Kundalini yogic science.

Breathing at a rate of 8 breaths per minute helps you:

- Feel more relaxed
- Relieve stress and increase mental awareness
- Activate the parasympathetic nervous system, which allows you to rest and digest
- Elevate healing processes

Breathing at a rate of 4 breaths per minute helps you:

- Experience positive shifts in mental function
- Have intense feelings of awareness, increased visual clarity, and heightened body sensitivity
- Enhance the coordination of pituitary and pineal glands, producing a meditative state

Breathing at a rate of 1 breath per minute helps you:

- Optimize cooperation between brain hemispheres
- Dramatically calm anxiety, fear, and worry
- Open to feel your presence and the presence of Spirit
- Develop intuition

"If you want things to be done for you, so you don't have to do anything, then you must breathe from one to five or six breaths per minute. If you can practice that, then you can attract the Universe to you. It is no secret. It's a simple thing. The longer and deeper your breath is, the more your psyche attracts everything to you — it's a way to prosperity." - Yogi Bhajan

Bonus Challenge: Set your day up with more breath every morning moving forward in the challenge. After following the meditation instructions from day one, take a minute to pause and breathe normally. Focus on the number of breaths you're taking per minute and and try to reduce the number each day. If you're experienced at breathwork, you can try the one-minute breath: Inhale for 20 seconds, hold for 20 seconds, exhale for 20 seconds and do this for 11 minutes. With this breathwork, Yogi Bhajan said, you will master your mind.

DAY 4: Get Grounded

Now that you're becoming more aware of your emotions and more mindful of your breath, we're going to take being present to a whole new level. See, being present is all about groundedness. When you're grounded, you can receive the gifts that the universe wants to give you. If you're high in the sky, like a hot pizza pie, you're not able to sustain higher vibrations, and you can't continue to grow.

Think of a tree in the forest. If it doesn't have strong roots, it will topple over and will only be able to grow so tall. The deeper you root into the earth, the higher you can fly.

Today, we're challenging you to get more grounded. We want you to really feel what this means and why it matters so much when it comes to raising your vibration. This is going to be so fun!

Grounding's not boring, promise.

Kundalini yoga isn't just about elevation and expansion. There are also kriyas — series of postures, breathing techniques, and sounds — designed for staying grounded. While grounding doesn't sound as fun as that Kundalini high everyone talks about, it's a vital part of elevating, as it allows you to be present in your body and present in the moment.

Need proof that grounding isn't a snooze-fest? Yogi Bhajan talks a lot about how the more grounded you are, the more money you'll have. The idea is that if you're both grounded and connected to the cosmos, you can receive divine guidance and also have the commitment to show up, take action, and birth things into the world — oh, hi abundance!

It isn't always easy on the healing path, especially when dealing with past traumas, deep emotions, family baggage, etc. Being grounded and utterly present with yourself is hard, as it forces you to confront the physical, mental, and emotional pain that hangs out in your body.

Some people go to great lengths to numb themselves from this feeling on a daily basis through their food choices, lifestyle, thoughts, and other distractions. This is why many people tend to gravitate more towards elevation and expansion — it makes it easier for us to ignore our shadows, which is where the term spiritual bypassing comes from. We don't see the point in spiritual bypassing, because if you get to a destination without actually healing, you won't be happy or fulfilled. (And you definitely won't be able to stay in a high-vibe place for too long.)

Focusing solely on the higher realms of consciousness can also be used to escape from the here and now. People may run from their present reality by moving into the higher energy centers — especially the 6th and 7th chakras — while avoiding the lower energy centers. This can result in a wild, ungrounded imagination and an overly developed intellect. An ungrounded imagination can cause an inability to see reality, whereas an overly developed intellect can cause you to live in your head.

It can take a lot to get grounded, especially when it's not your natural MO. Being grounded in the root chakra means that you feel *everything*. Yeah, that can be rough sometimes, but it's the first step to actually discovering what you need to work on and heal.

If you learn to flex your grounding muscles on command, it'll be easier for you to move through the chaos in daily life without losing your footing. You may find healing is quicker, and you'll have the foundation that'll allow you to explore those higher chakra realms in a balanced way.

7 Amazing Grounding Tools We Love*

1. Eat salty foods or even have some Himalayan pink salt directly. Avoid sweets as they're more yin and won't help keep you grounded.

2. Eat grounding foods such as root vegetables and beets.

3. Contract or send your awareness to the root lock (mulbandh), which is your rectum, sex organs, and navel point. This is where the Root Chakra is located. It can also be helpful to visualize a square and the color red.

4. Meditate with the tongue tip at the back of the lower teeth and slightly push the whole tongue to the floor of your mouth. This will ground you.

5. Consciously feel your feet on the ground as you walk or stand. Try not to sit with your feet off of the floor. Walk barefoot on sand, dirt, grass, or concrete at least once a day.

6. Take a walk in nature and pay attention to the scent of dirt, leaves, and wood. (Earthy smells are very grounding.)

7. Do a Kundalini yoga posture or meditation for the root chakra. A great quick Kundalini Yoga posture to try for grounding and the root is this variation of crow pose.

Crow Pose: Begin standing and bring the feet a little wider than hip-width distance apart. Turn the toes outward. Interlace the fingers, except for the index finger and straighten the arms, so the fingers point straight ahead, and your arms are parallel to the ground. Elbows are straight. Slowly lower down into a squat, hips coming all the way down by the ankles if possible. Focus out beyond the horizon and begin long, slow, deep breathing. Arms stay parallel to the ground as you continue to move upwards and downwards. Let your inhales move down to the base of the spine, filling this area with vitality, and with your exhales release any tension or blockages you may feel. Practice for 1-3 minutes.

TODAY'S CHALLENGE

Choose and try one of the above grounding practices or play the below game.

An easy — and fun! — way to get grounded is to play the "5-4-3-2-1" game. Do this at least once today in a moment when you're feeling stressed.

- **Name 5** things you can see in the room with you.
- **Name 4** things you can feel ("chair on my back" or "feet on the floor")
- **Name 3** things you can hear ("fingers tapping on the keyboard" or "TV")
- **Name 2** things you can smell (or 2 things you like the smell of)
- **Name 1** good thing about yourself

Journal how you feel after you practiced the grounding tool or played this game. Anything new you noticed? Any thoughts or ideas that came up?

_____

_____

_____

_____

_____

Bonus Challenge: Practice Crow Pose mentioned above in the 7 amazing grounding tools we love for 1-3 minutes. You are doing fantastic, remember that!! Keep it up!!

DAY 5: Balance Your Chakras

Today let's talk about how the energy works inside of this high-performance vehicle our souls are riding in ... our bodies.

We have 8 energy centers in our bodies called chakras.

These centers are physical locations where the most nerve endings come together and energy gathers. Each chakra is connected to different organs, aspects of our lives, and frequencies that determine our total frequency.

These energy centers also make up our aura (the 8th chakra), which is the electromagnetic field of energy around us. This field attracts and repels things in and out of our lives.

If any of your 8 energy centers are closed or out of balance, then the energy within your body can't flow in harmony. This leads to lower-vibration emotions because our bodies have somewhat of an energy dam clogging up the system. The energy can't move freely or as quickly, and it causes disharmony in our bodies, minds, thoughts, and emotions.

But when our chakras are in balance, and the energy can flow openly between them, we're able to control our moods and fully manifest whatever it is that we want. Our bodies remain healthy and youthful because our blood is flowing, our organs are oxygenated, our minds are clear, and our systems are working at their best. From that place, we feel good, and everything works together. Our actions align with our high soul path. Sounds pretty great, huh?

TODAY'S CHALLENGE

Quiz time! We're going to figure out how balanced your chakras are and help you to become more aware of any imbalances and opportunities for healing.

Circle the attributes you experience — if you've circled more under the "imbalanced" section than in the "balanced" section, that chakra may be out of balance.

THE LOWER TRIANGLE - ENERGIES OF "ME"

Root - 1st Chakra
YOUR SECURITY + SURVIVAL CENTER

BALANCED

1. Secure with yourself
2. A sense of belonging on the Earth
3. You feel stable
4. Life flows with ease
5. Loose grip on attachments
6. Financial abundance
7. Not focused on fear
8. Satisfying sex life

IMBALANCED

1. Life feels like a burden
2. Feeling like you don't belong
3. Anxiety disorders
4. Overly fearful
5. Nightmares
6. Problems with elimination organs (and prostate in men)
7. Physical and mental resistance
8. Sex drive is on hyperdrive

Sacral - 2nd Chakra
YOUR CREATIVITY CENTER

BALANCED

1. You feel positive about life
2. Expressing emotions is easy and comfortable
3. You feel in control of your life
4. Relaxed attitude towards sex
5. Healthy sexual organ function
6. Expressing patience is easy
7. Creativity flows to you easily
8. A healthy attitude towards relationships

IMBALANCED

1. Not comfortable showing emotion or feeling emotionally numb
2. Being *overly* emotional or ruled by your emotions
3. Lack of boundaries with others
4. Codependency in relationships
5. Addictive behaviors
6. Overindulgence in sexual fantasies or lack of sexual desire
7. Problems with reproductive organs
8. Hip, lower back, or lower abdominal pain

Solar Plexus - 3rd Chakra
YOUR ACTION + BALANCE CENTER

BALANCED

1. Commitment is easy
2. Healthy self-esteem
3. A strong sense of purpose
4. You feel confident
5. Self-motivated and proactive
6. You can rely on yourself
7. You're responsible
8. Healthy, smooth digestive function

IMBALANCED

1. You carry a lot of anger
2. Controlling behavior
3. Low self-esteem and insecurity
4. Feelings of despair
5. Difficulty making decisions
6. Everything is an obstacle
7. Fatigue or excessive laziness
8. Problems with digestive organs, constipation

> BALANCE POINT - "ME" BECOMES "WE"
> WHERE THE ENERGIES OF THE LOWER TRIANGLE + THE UPPER TRIANGLE MEET

Heart - 4th Chakra
YOUR LOVE + COMPASSION CENTER

BALANCED

1. You feel love and compassion for yourself and others
2. Empathy
3. Kindness
4. You appreciate beauty in all things
5. Stable, deep and meaningful relationships
6. Ability to forgive and accept
7. Spiritual awareness
8. Healthy hormone function

IMBALANCED

1. Attachment to people and things, codependency
2. Feeling closed down
3. Overly defensive and easily hurt
4. Not being able to forgive others
5. Fearing intimacy
6. People pleasing, helper syndrome
7. Isolation and antisocial behavior
8. Heart, lung, or blood pressure problems

THE UPPER TRIANGLE - ENERGIES OF "WE"

Throat - 5th Chakra
YOUR PROJECTIVE POWER CENTER

BALANCED

1. You're comfortable speaking out and expressing your truth
2. Ability to listen and communicate effectively
3. Connection to spirit and intuitive abilities
4. Authenticity
5. Ability to teach and inspire others
6. Your voice projects into a room
7. Realizing your purpose
8. Healthy thyroid function

IMBALANCED

1. Lack of control over your speech and what you say to others
2. Not being able to listen to others
3. Excessive fear of speaking
4. Low, quiet voice that does not project
5. Telling lies
6. Excessive shyness
7. Voice problems
8. Insecurity or fear of other people's opinions and judgments

Third Eye - 6th Chakra
YOUR INTUITION, WISDOM + IDENTITY CENTER

BALANCED

1. You can visualize what you want in life
2. Connection to your intuition
3. Self-initiation
4. You perceive subtle dimensions and movements of energy
5. Psychic abilities are open and developed (or developing), especially clairvoyance (seeing) and clairaudience (hearing)
6. You have insight into your life and others'

IMBALANCED

1. Lack of clarity or confusion
2. Feeling stuck and not able to envision a new life
3. Depression
4. Rejection of spirituality
5. Over-intellectualizing everything
6. Not being able to see the greater picture

Crown - 7th Chakra
YOUR TENTH GATE

BALANCED

1. Aware of higher consciousness and wisdom
2. Not stuck in limiting patterns
3. Feeling limitless
4. Communication with higher states of consciousness
5. Experiencing unity with the divine
6. You're comfortable with the unknown
7. Ability to surrender

IMBALANCED

1. Disconnected from spirit
2. Constantly being pessimistic
3. Feeling separate from existence or out of your body
4. Headaches
5. Obsessive attachment to spirituality
6. Being closed-minded
7. Fearing death

Aura - 8th Chakra
YOUR ELECTROMAGNETIC FIELD

BALANCED

1. Feeling strong and energized
2. Feeling vibrant, bright, and radiant
3. Feeling protected

IMBALANCED

1. Feeling shy and withdrawn
2. Feeling dull, weak, or vulnerable
3. You have an illness

Figuring out where you're imbalanced is the first step towards working to balance your chakras. There are lots of ways to do this. Kundalini yoga and meditation and a diet to support all the chakras together is the most effective way we've found to balance the chakras fast (and for the long term)! It's wild how we've been able to transform our health and personal issues through this work.

If you're interested in going deeper with your chakra knowledge, we have a whole podcast episode dedicated to the chakras - Episode 13 "RISE UP: Everything You Need to Know About Your Chakras + Allowing Yourself to Live a High-Vibrational Life". Head over to your favorite podcast platform to listen. You can also find it on our site elevatetheglobe.com/podcast.

To give you a start, we wanted to share a few foods that are great for each chakra that you can start to incorporate more of into your diet to balance your system.

Root - 1st Chakra	Root Vegetables like Beets + Potatoes
Sacral - 2nd Chakra	Carrots + Squash
Solar Plexus - 3rd Chakra	Complex Carbohydrates, Lemons, Bananas
Heart - 4th Chakra	Leafy Greens
Throat - 5th Chakra	Fruits that grow on trees like Apples + Pears
Third Eye - 6th Chakra	Nuts, Seeds + Legumes
Crown - 7th Chakra	Lots of water + eating light meals that don't weigh you down

cleansing

DAY 6: Do a Brain Dump

You've done some incredible work so far! You're making small shifts in your mindset and bringing in stress-management tools, like grounding and breathwork, that will start to create big change. These small steps in the right direction will take you on a whole new path. BRAVO! Be sure to give yourself a lot of love for showing up for your future self. It's not always easy, but it's worth it.

Today, we're going to practice something that sounds gross, but that will create beautiful changes in your life: brain dumping. Top CEOs recommend doing this once a day as a mini-detox for your mind, and we agree it's a powerful tool.

See, a lot of times we lose trust in ourselves because we aren't connected to our own truth. Instead, we're connected to the junkie-junk in our minds that came from other people. Maybe it's from your parents' idea that you have to work hard and hate your job to have money. Or you may have false beliefs about your body from that kid who made fun of you in 5th grade.

Remember how we said that whatever you think about creates the dominant vibration you're attracting from? Brain dumping is a way to tidy your conscious thoughts — it's a mental shower. (And it's especially effective if you pair it with meditation to clean up your subconscious vibration.)

TODAY'S CHALLENGE

Write out anything on your mind — anything you think about often that bugs or worries you, or something you keep forgetting to do.

It can be something you think about at night or in the car or while you're on the treadmill at the gym. Let's get all the shit out, this is a colonic for the mind!

_____

_____

_____

_____

_____

_____

_____

_____

_____

Now that you've gotten all these things out of your head look at them. Are these beliefs about yourself or your situation even true? Are these thoughts necessary? Are they kind? If a thought you've listed is none of these things, cross it off the list. If it *is* one of these things, put your energy into addressing it.

We want you to start using this filter whenever a thought comes to mind - *Is it true, is it kind, is it necessary?*

So many times, we waste precious energy on things that are not true, kind, or necessary. This is energy that could go into more important things, like creating yourself a new reality, living a high purpose, feeling your best, helping to elevate the globe and doing cool stuff in the world. You know, the things you are here on this planet to do.

The last step is to speak kindly with yourself. We have listed affirmation suggestions below, or you can write some for yourself.
Select 1-3 that resonate for you and write them down.

Next, practice using your voice and say them out loud. We know this can be uncomfortable or downright scary, but it's so important to use our voice and to create new patterns. Let's do this!

I AM LIGHT
I AM BEAUTIFUL.
I AM LOVED.
I AM LOVE.
I AM MAGICAL.
I HAVE EVERYTHING I NEED.
I AM WORTHY.
I AM RADIANT.
I AM A POWERFUL CO-CREATOR WITH THE UNIVERSE.
I HAVE UNLIMITED ENERGY AVAILABLE TO ME.
I AM LIMITLESS.
I AM A POWERFUL MAGNET ATTRACTING EVERYTHING I WANT TO ME.

Write down your own affirmations here, if you want:

_____

_____

_____

Bonus Challenge: List everything in your life that stresses you out and then rank each one on a scale from one (least stressful) to ten (most stressful).

Apply the true-kind-necessary test from the above challenge. It's important to realize some of these stressful things we tell ourselves are not true, and we can shift our perception and how we think about them.

Beside each stressor, can you think of any solutions to lower the stress? Is it an action or a shift in perception?

If it's an action, great! Take action today with at least one solution, or create a new perception, a new way of looking at your stressor, and begin to speak your new perception out loud to yourself today. Practice being aware of ways you can reduce your stress. (Hint, hint: The morning breathwork from Day 3 and any meditation is super helpful because it actually changes the stress response in your body chemistry).

Example Stressor: Commute to Work with Traffic

Solutions to lower stress: Ride-share; listen to a podcast or audiobook; go earlier and work out a couple days a week; practice long deep breathing in your car; listen to mantras; ask your boss if you can come in earlier and leave earlier or work from home one day a week to lower your stress and be more productive.

A change in perception could be that your commute is your "me" time and you get to fill it up with practices (deep breathing), mantras that change your brainwaves, and information (audiobooks/podcasts) that accelerate your life and your spiritual growth. It's your sacred time!

There are so many options for every problem! Anything that's clogging your mind, bugging you, or always a problem, let's get rid of it!

REMINDER: Go over to www.elevatetheglobe.com/21dayelevatehighertoolkit and press play to practice a meditation video with us! Keep meditating every day or as much as possible! If we were next to you, we would give you a big HELL YEAH hug, because brain dumping is a big deal :) Keep moving, you've got this!

DAY 7: Clean Up Your Crew

How do you feel after finding solutions for your stressors and consciously being kinder to yourself? Pretty fab, right?

Well, now that you're practicing all of these positive tools yourself, it's time to realize you're not alone here on the planet! (Haha!) While sometimes it might feel more comfortable to do this work alone — and sometimes it's necessary — we all want and need human connection, and we all deserve to have amazing people in our lives. So today is all about looking at your environment and the people around you because these things also have a major influence on your reality and your vibration!

Your tribe affects your vibe.

You've probably heard countless times that you are most like the 5 people you surround yourself with. It's true that your friends, family, and co-workers largely impact how you feel and what your current reality looks like. And it's not just the people you interact with IRL. A recent article* in *National Geographic* mentioned that the people you friend and follow online also shape your experience of the world, even if you've never met them.

"How we experience the world is intensely shaped by who and what we surround ourselves with on a daily basis. Today that can include more virtual, social media friends than real ones." - Agustin Fuentes, *National Geographic**

We want to help you clear out anybody who's bringing down your vibration on the regular — or shift those relationships to a higher caliber, so they're not just about gossiping or watching *Real Housewives* together. LOL! No judgment here, but if you want to elevate your life, engaging with things or people that constantly bring you down will delay the process.

Here's the thing: Some people may never be ready to rise at the same time as you are. The worst thing you can do is try to force your beliefs upon someone, so in these cases, you may feel called to spend less time with them.

We know this can sometimes be difficult with family, close friends, or colleagues. Often lightworkers are put into familial groups to help people wake up, so if your family is different than you or on another path, just know it's normal. You can start to create energetic boundaries. For example, when a specific low-vibration conversation comes up, you might switch the topic or choose not to engage. It may not be letting go of someone altogether, but letting go of a particular aspect of your relationship.

For example ...

Let's say you have a friend who always wants to go to the bar and gossip, and it always leaves you feeling depleted and low-vibe. Could you ask her to go to a yoga class or hike instead? If not, it might be time to limit your interactions.

Only you know what is right here. Don't feel any pressure to do anything drastic, like cut people out of your life on a dime. Just start to be more aware and look at where you can do some relational cleansing! Sometimes, the smallest shift can put a relationship on a new course and make you feel better, opening up space for a new or different relationship to flourish.

Your hardest relationships are your biggest teachers.

The second part of this is realizing that everyone we encounter is a mirror, allowing us to look at ourselves from a different perspective. Often times, there's a lesson or opportunity for growth when we feel low-vibe emotions towards someone.

The first Sutra of Yogi Bhajan's 5 Sutras of the Aquarian Age is: Recognize that the other person is you. We're gonna dive deeper into what this means in today's challenge, but we love this explanation by Haribhajan Singh:

We can only truly see ourselves reflected in another person. If we admire qualities in another, we are only seeing those same qualities in ourselves. These qualities may not yet be developed or expressed. On the flip side, if we see qualities that we dislike in another — again, we are only seeing ourselves — perhaps a disowned part called the shadow.

The more we identify with our ego, the more judgmental we will be toward others and the more we will project our own personality traits onto others.

In the Age of Aquarius, the age of enlightenment, we are being called to take full responsibility for our experiences and to live the Truth — we are ALL ONE." - Haribhajan Singh

TODAY'S CHALLENGE

We're going to do a meditation to align you with the idea that "the other person is you." Then, you're going to look at all of your relationships — both real-life and virtual — to figure out which ones make you feel good, and which ones aren't as aligned."

Then there are, of course, times when there is toxic energy that you need to remove yourself from. But we also want to look at how we can OWN what we see in another person and use it to grow.

Kundalini Meditation: 1st Sutra Meditation
INSTRUCTIONS

Tune In - Before we begin any Kundalini Meditation, we always tune in with the Adi Mantra 3 times to connect with the wisdom within us and protect our energy.

Bring your hands together in prayer pose, thumb tips touching your sternum, press the palms together and close the eyes. Inhale and chant "Ong Namo, Guru Dev Namo" 3 times.

Open your eyes and begin the Meditation by following the directions below.

Posture/Mudra - Sit in Easy Pose with a straight spine. Place your right elbow at your side against your ribcage and make a fist with your right hand with the Jupiter finger (index finger) pointing up. Your fist should be next to your face. Place your left hand over the heart center. You can also do this meditation sitting back to back with a partner.

Focus - Close the eyes and focus your gaze inward and up between the brow point (your third eye).

Mantra - *Humee Hum, Tumee Tum, Wahe Guru; I am Thine, in Mine, Myself, Wahe Guru*

Chant with the Humee Hum mp3 for 11 minutes. Humee huh?!

If that's what you're thinking, get the scoop on this mantra from Gurucharan Singh Khalsa, director of training at Kundalini Research Institute.

EXCERPT: Sutra One + the Humee Hum Mantra*

Humee huh?! If that's what you're thinking, get the scoop on this mantra from Gurucharan Singh Khalsa, director of training at Kundalini Research Institute. A sutra is a statement that weaves together two realms — the finite and the Infinite — into the consciousness that supports the Self. This sutra — *Recognize the other person is you* — has three dimensions: I, You and Thou/Infinite.

The sutra says that you and every person share a common nucleus; a still point that is by nature infinite. It is both before and beyond our ordinary sense of time and space and yet gives birth to all that is experienced in time and space. It is similar to what physicists call the quantum vacuum. It is an empty stillness from which all things arise. We enter that by creating a state of *shuniya* in meditation and prayer.

As that Oneness expresses, it takes the form of polarities. A basic polarity is you and others. You and me. Without stillness and depth in our heart, these seem different, opposed or unrelated. **But as we attune to the depth within our own consciousness (Humee Hum) and listen to the depth in the other person (Tumee Tum) and place both sensitivities before the Infinite (Wahe Guru), we are multiplied.**

The mantra we are using with this sutra — *Humee Hum, Tumee Tum, Wahe Guru; I am Thine, in Mine, Myself, Wahe Guru* — has a subtle structure in its sound, beat, and arrangement. We vibrate it from within our heart and listen to our sound and become merged in it. There is a 3.5 cycle energetic rhythm in this chant. This does not mean just the beat or the *tal*. It means the energetic gesture of the chant in meaning, energy, and projection.

To sense and manifest the subtle insight of this sutra, there is no stronger affirmation than *Humee Hum, Tumee Tum, Wahe Guru; I am Thine, in Mine, Myself, Wahe Guru.* In this way, clarity of mind comes. The sense of personal purpose and life purpose comes. And a profound connectedness with other people and with All that Is arises.

51

Once you've finished the meditation, complete the following journal prompts:

Notice the giving and receiving balance between you and your closest crew. How do you feel after you interact with each person? Do you feel uplifted or do you feel energetically depleted?

_____

_____

_____

_____

_____

_____

_____

_____

Do the same with social media. How do you feel after you watch someone's stories or see their posts? Do you feel uplifted or do you feel weighed down?

_____

_____

_____

_____

_____

_____

_____

_____

_____

_____

Make a list of people or social media accounts that make you feel guilt, shame, fear, jealousy, or just don't make you feel good.

Look at why you might feel this way. Are there qualities in these other people that you actually want to embody yourself, like their confidence or their abundance? Or is there something about them that you're judging — and maybe you're also judging that part of yourself, deep down? See if you can find the root of where these negative emotions are coming from within you, and journal about the insights you can take away from these feelings.

_____

_____

_____

_____

_____

_____

_____

_____

List what you're going to do about these connections.

You could have a talk with them to see if you can change your perspective of the connection — you might be surprised at how it shifts your interactions. On the other hand, you could also create stronger boundaries by spending less time with them or unfollowing them online.

_____

_____

_____

_____

_____

_____

_____

_____

_____

DAY 8: Detox Your Media Diet

Today we're piggybacking on yesterday, but diving a little deeper than just people. We're almost done with cleansing and clearing energetic blocks *out* of our body, but we can't forget about what we're taking in. Everything we consume affects our vibration, for better or for worse.

Think back a few days ago to our chat about $E=MC^2$ and the Law of Vibration. Both of these laws proved that everything is energy resonating at a specific vibratory frequency or pattern. This includes everything we take in with our senses. When you're consuming lower-vibrational content — music, TV shows, magazines, art — you're aligning your reality in the same frequency with these things.

Plus, everything around you is being imprinted on your subconscious mind, which if you remember, drives your actions. It's why the multi-billion dollar companies pay to have billboards and commercials everywhere. They know if you see a McDonald's hamburger enough, your subconscious mind will crave it.

If we let ourselves be driven by what surrounds us, then we are essentially robots who aren't in control of our lives and most likely not living our high paths. Say you're always listening to songs about people cheating and shows full of violence, drama, and more violence ... guess what your subconscious will be filled with? You guessed it, all of that shit. Then you wonder why you are constantly jealous and questioning your boyfriend or feeling afraid of the world around you. (But don't judge yourself — this negative energy is all around you! Of course you would be feeling this way.)

On the flip side, do you want to travel the world, find a love deeper than no other, find your dream BFF, or manifest that peak performance, car, money, and house you want? Follow and interact with media and people who have and are doing those things, and surround yourself with positive music, shows, books, and messaging. These people and things can expand our belief in what's possible and show us things we can manifest. Consuming these types of media will take you higher up the scale vs. dragging you down. Feel us?

We personally don't watch much standard TV at all at this point, but we love to engage in positive, inspiring media content. We are just really selective about what we consume because it's made an enormous difference in our lives. We love to watch documentaries that expand our mind (we love the ones on Gaia.com).

The magic of "consuming" mantras

We also love to listen and chant along to the high-vibrational sacred sound of the Kundalini mantras (we love White Sun and had the lead singer Gurujas on our podcast — check out episode 44!). We know mantras can feel super strange to listen to at first, let alone chant. But once you release the fear and self-consciousness, chanting is the best thing ever, in our opinion! Why is it so magical? When we chant, we are tapping on particular parts of the upper palate of the mouth, with a specific sequence and rhythm that's believed to set off a chemical reaction in the brain and cells. It unlocks doors to higher levels of consciousness that allow us to connect and manifest through and with the divine. It's called Naad Science if you want to look into it further.

"Mantras are the mind vibration in relationship to the Cosmos. The science of mantra is based on the knowledge that sound is a form of energy having structure, power, and a definite predictable effect on the human psyche...Mantra takes the vibratory effect of each of your molecules into the Infinity of the Cosmos." -Yogi Bhajan

Remember, our vibratory frequency is directly related to the frequencies we are surrounded by — and our frequency determines our level of consciousness and our overall physical, mental and emotional health. Mantras are just another easy tool to keep our frequency sky-high.

TODAY'S CHALLENGE

Think of one type of media you consume that isn't in the high-vibrational energy that you want to be in. Take it out of your life for just today and replace it with a mantra.

Play the mantra on repeat, at low volume (barely audible is fine!), while you work or in the car. Bonus points if you chant along or play the mantra while you sleep. The beauty of playing mantras while you sleep is that the high-frequency sound current can slip through your conscious mind and into your subconscious mind, helping to reshape and repattern it, without you having to do anything!

If you don't have a mantra you love, you can start with **Ek Ong Kar Sat Gur Prasad.** This mantra is all about removing and shifting any negative energy and getting rid of any blocks in your way.* We love the version by Jai-Jagdeesh — it's on our Spotify playlist, found in the 21 Day Challenge Tool Kit.

Here's what Yogi Bhajan had to say about Ek Ong Kar Sat Gur Prasad:

"This mantra elevates the self beyond duality and establishes the flow of the spirit. It will remove all obstacles."

Complete the following journal prompts at some point today:

What are you deciding to take out of your life for just one day?

At the end of the day, how did it feel without this in your life?

_____

_____

_____

_____

_____

_____

_____

_____

Don't forget to share your experience with a friend or in the Facebook group!

This is getting real, you are starting to really make major moves babe!! If someone hasn't told you yet today, we just have to say, YOU ROCK!

DAY 9: Clear The Clutter

You are moving on up and raising your vibration, even if you can't feel it yet. Or maybe you're feeling it a lot, and everything in your life is starting to shift. Either way, our goal is to help you clear absolutely everything that could be stopping you from the massive elevation and growth you're about to experience. So today, we're going to look at your clutter situation.

Making room for abundance

Have you ever heard that your outer surroundings are a reflection of your inner state? For energy to flow and circulate, it needs space. When your car is messy, your sink's full of dishes, and your closet's a mess, there's simply not enough room for positive energy to come in.

It is not by chance that any movie depicting wealth is filled with immaculate homes and cars, clean purses, clean shoes, and lots of open space. It's also not by chance that hoarders live in fear, thinking they can't get rid of anything because then they might not get anything new. It's actually the opposite — when you let go of attachments to things that you don't need (hello balanced root chakra!), you make space for new energy and abundance to flow into your life effortlessly.

If you hold on to something too tightly, it weighs you down, clogs your mind, and blocks you from receiving anything new. And we know you're looking for *all new everything* in the life of your wildest dreams.

TODAY'S CHALLENGE

Clear out a physical space in your life. Let's start small: Maybe it's your wallet, your car, your desk, your desktop on your computer, your email inbox, your closet, your bathroom cabinet, etc. The one that feels most important to clean out is the one to choose today.

You don't have to finish one entire area today. Just start cleaning it up and creating space. For example, if it's your car you want to clean up but it's overwhelming to even start, just clear out the backseat.

If you can identify multiple areas that feel important to cleanse, think about each one and pinpoint the emotion that arises on the Emotional Scale. Which area is vibrating the lowest on the scale? Tackle that one first.

What space are you going to clean out today?

_____

Complete the following journal prompts at some point today:

How do you feel?

_____

_____

_____

_____

_____

What is your relationship to clutter and how do you feel about your clutter situation? Allow yourself to free write and put down anything that comes through.

DAY 10: Ditch The Toxins

The Elevate the Globe lifestyle is all about protecting our health, feeling our best, and being part of the solution that will create a better world for everyone. It's a huge job, but one place we can *all* make a difference is in our cabinets.

We've learned so much about the chemicals present in clothing and beauty products — they affect our health (and the health of the planet) in many ways. According to a 2007 study by the Environmental Working Group, 1 in 5 personal care products contain chemicals linked to cancer, while 80% contain ingredients that may have dangerous impurities.* And in 2015, Swedish researchers also found high toxin levels in 60 items of clothing, including chemicals that can cause cancer and pollute the water.*

We love clothing that is hand-dyed in small batches using natural pigments. Not only is this healthier for Mother Earth and us, but in many cases, the people making the clothes have a better quality of life and better working conditions than other garment industry workers. (Slave labor is still prevalent and affects not only the people in the situation but also the energy on the planet.)

We also look for beauty and cleaning products that are made with only non-toxic ingredients, because we don't want our physical body or our physical spaces to be filled with harmful chemicals.

And there are so many other easy ways to reduce toxins in the home, specifically. We love to open the windows every day to let fresh air in — it's one of the easiest, cheapest ways to circulate and cleanse the air in your home. We learned about how many toxins are tracked in the home through our shoes, so we started taking off our shoes at the door. We also love to sage ourselves and the house regularly. If you are new to saging, check out the video on our Youtube channel, Elevate the Globe TV and found in the 21 Day Challenge Tool Kit.

"Indoor air can have higher concentrations of toxins than outdoor air. Ironically, these chemical toxins come from the products we use to make our lives better." — Greg Seaman, founder of Eartheasy

TODAY'S CHALLENGE

Do one thing to start cleansing your home of toxins. You can open your windows, start taking your shoes off in the house, sage, or switch out some of your products.

If you're called to start using cleaner personal-care products, choose one product that you're already using and see how it ranks on the Environmental Working Group's Skin Deep Cosmetics Database*. (You can also select a cleaning product and search for it on the EWG's Guide to Healthy Cleaning app). If it's rated as being of moderate-to-high concern regarding chemical content, make a plan to dump it for a healthier option.

For more resources go to the 21 Day Challenge Tool Kit for a list of our fav non-toxic products.

Wow, your energy is feeling cleaner by the day ... feeling major Oprah vibes from you! Tomorrow is so fun, see you then!

DAY 11: Elevate Your Pantry

We've been doing some serious cleansing over here ... you didn't know you were getting yourself into a detox, did you? LOL

Let's recap: You cleansed your mind and body of stressors with the brain dump. You opened up space to let new energy in by physically cleaning your space and re-evaluating your relationships and your media consumption. Plus, you started to rid your home of toxins. So what could you possibly have left to cleanse? Well, we've got one more big one, my friends...and we need you to head to the kitchen.

Open up your refrigerator and your cupboards. What the heck is inside? "You are what you eat" is not a mindless statement. If you're consuming junk food, your organs are filled with junk, and your vibration will also be filled with junk.

If you had a Maserati, would you put regular unleaded gas in there? No fucking way. The high-quality gas gives your car the peak performance that you paid for. If you put in low-quality fuel, your Maserati won't work as it's built to work.

You are just like the Maserati. If you want to raise your vibration, but the fuel you're feeding your body is like low-grade gasoline, how can you possibly stay in a high-vibrational place?

It might sound like something a cheesy bodybuilder from the 90s would say, but our bodies really are our temples. They are our vehicles here on planet Earth. They are our "meat suits" as we've heard it called. If your body isn't performing at its best, then your life won't reflect peak experiences, either.

Food is Energy

Just like all other matter, food vibrates at an array of frequencies. Kirlian photography actually can show us the energetic auras of different types of food. (And, as you can imagine, an apple looks way different than dead animal meat.)

If you've ever eaten something and soon felt energized and rejuvenated, got a second wind, or a burst of fire inside, then your food likely had a high-frequency life force that affected your own vibration.

Your body is smart, and it tells you what's up. If you don't feel good after eating something, then it's probably not good for your body, and it's affecting your mind and spirit as well.

The Food-Mood Connection

We've studied a lot about the food we eat and how it affects our brain, and there is a direct correlation. There have been countless scientific studies proving the link between food and our mood and emotions. Most of them show that anxiety, depression, lethargy, irritability, and cravings are linked to a poor or imbalanced diet.

Psychotherapist and spiritual teacher Doreen Virtue, the author of *Constant Cravings,* explains how cravings for food are a sign that the body and the emotions are looking for peace or homeostasis. They can stem from emotional or physical imbalances and have a big impact on our overall vibration.

'Intuitively, the body knows that certain foods will alter the brain chemicals or blood pressure in order to regulate energy or mood." — Doreen Virtue

There is so much we could go into here, but food is a sensitive subject — and it can also be complicated because everyone's body chemistry is different. But we find that looking at what we eat is key to getting to the root of understanding our mental and emotional states. Our food cravings give us information. When we're aware of an imbalance, we can shift what we eat, using food to change our thoughts and elevate our emotions to a higher vibration.

TODAY'S CHALLENGE

It's time to start a food/mood journal!

This will help you really begin to understand how certain foods make you feel and get to the root of what your food cravings are telling you. As you raise your awareness, you'll begin to understand what's best for *you*, as we're all different and no one way of eating works for everyone.

Here's what you're going to do:

1. Every time you eat something today, write out what you ate and how you felt before and after.

What I Ate | How I Felt

MEAL:	TIME:	BEFORE:	AFTER:
MEAL:	TIME:	BEFORE:	AFTER:
MEAL:	TIME:	BEFORE:	AFTER:
MEAL:	TIME:	BEFORE:	AFTER:
MEAL:	TIME:	BEFORE:	AFTER:
MEAL:	TIME:	BEFORE:	AFTER:
MEAL:	TIME:	BEFORE:	AFTER:
MEAL:	TIME:	BEFORE:	AFTER:

2. Then, look at everything you ate and determine what taste profile it falls under. Traditional Chinese Medicine links cravings for specific tastes to organ imbalances, which are outlined here. We can focus on the corresponding chakras with Kundalini Yoga and meditation to help ourselves heal from the inside out.

Chakra	Craving	What You Need	What You Should Eat Instead
HEART 4th Heart Chakra	**Bitter** coffee, chocolate, caffeine	Magnesium, Iron, Phosphate	raw cacao, nuts, arugula, brussels sprouts, swiss chard, artichokes
LIVER 3rd Solar Plexus Chakra	**Sour** sour candy, lemon/citrus, sourdough bread, vinegar/fermented foods	Nitrogen	high protein, chia seeds, blueberries, red beets, tomatoes, artichokes
KIDNEY 2nd Sacral Chakra	**Salty** extra salt on meals, salty crunchy chips, cheese	Chloride Silicon	healthy fats, almond butter, coconut/nut milk, cashews, nuts, seeds, goji berries, seaweed
LUNG 4th Heart Chakra	**Pungent + Spicy** spicy food, hot sauce, OR pungent mints/gum	Lower Body Temperature	green onion, pepper, garlic, ginger, chili
SPLEEN OR STOMACH 2nd + 3rd Chakras	**Sweet** sugar, grains, dairy, candy	Chromium, Carbon, Phosphorus, Sulphur, Trytophan	celery, carrots, winter squash, sweet potatoes, brown rice, dates

BONUS: PORTION SIZE TIP

We get a lot of questions about portion size, and we believe in only eating until we feel ¾ full, because our brains need a minute to catch up to how full our stomachs are.

If you feel stuffed, you're overeating and will feel low-energy because you're clogging your system. Be aware that switching to a new, healthier diet could cause some discomfort, as your body needs time to adjust to eating new foods. But beyond that, you can look to how you feel as a measurement for what's best for your body.

Okay, we feel like your energetic pantry (and possibly your physical one) is looking way cleaner... wow, you are on fire!!! See you manana to get into some money hacks.

DAY 12: Patch Up Money Leaks

One last piece of the cleansing puzzle before we completely wrap it up! We want to be thorough here, so this is the last checkpoint to make sure there are no holes in the boat — especially when it comes to money, which is a considerable source of energy in our lives.

You might be feeling confused, like, "What are you talking about, leaks? Leaks in the bathtub?"

We're talking about places in your life force energy, also known as chi, that are being drained. Chi is another word for the energy vibrating in your body and energy field, and if it's leaking out in certain areas, it will feel depleting in different ways. If you have energetic leaks, it's normal to feel tired all the time, be easily distracted, have trouble getting tasks done, feel unorganized or overwhelmed, and feel like money disappears quickly and you don't know where it goes. You can feel like you're working really hard, but nothing is moving forward.

We've talked about the ways clutter, toxic relationships, and other areas of life can drain our energy, so for today, we want to focus on any financial leaks you may be experiencing. (But if additional leaks become conscious here, feel free to write them down and address them in the same way!)

Money is energy.

Like everything else, money follows the Law of Mentalism. What you believe and feel about it dictates the experience you'll have with it. Here are some common causes of money leaks, some of which we've talked about already:

- Ignoring or worrying about money all the time
- Spending money where you don't want to in order to please others
- Fear-based thinking around money — like thinking it's going to leave you
- Clutter in your wallet, desk, or place where you pay bills or work on your finances
- Complaining and wanting things to be different than they are — not appreciating where you are now
- Distracting yourself with social media or things outside of yourself, like reality TV — not really living your own life
- Substance abuse (drugs, alcohol, or smoking) and wasting money on other addictive, low-vibe behaviors
- Never saying no to things because of FOMO

You can measure where you're at with money by the emotions you feel about it. No matter where that may be, we want you to be aware of it. And remember, you can always make it better!

TODAY'S CHALLENGE

We're going to find any energetic money leaks you need to mend. We encourage you to create space around your finances weekly if possible and whenever you're working with your finances make it fun — light a candle, play some mantras, grab a tea, whatever feels good to you. "

1. Money Review

Go through your bank statement for the last month and look at any places money is unnecessarily draining out. Take note of how you feel about it. Even if you just look at a few line items today and come back to it, let's get into the energy of elevating your money vibes!

Here are some examples of money leaks:

- Are you spending money on things you aren't using — subscriptions, magazines or music? Either start using it or cancel.

- Are there parking tickets you haven't paid that are racking up fees?

- Do you buy a bunch of food you never eat that ends up going to waste? Start a grocery list or grocery delivery service and only buy what you know you'll eat. Plan to make a soup or get creative to use up anything that will go to waste.

- Are you getting expensive coffees, teas, juices, or smoothies you could make at home that would make you feel more abundant?

- Do you have any credit card or loan interest that's too high? Usually by calling you can get your interest rate lowered. Or look at switching to a cash back or better rewards credit/debit card.

- Do you have uncashed checks sitting around? Unused or partially unused gift cards? Unclaimed refunds and rebates? Any money you're ignoring and not giving love and respect to?

- Are you undercharging for your products or services? If you're undervaluing your time, you're leaking money as well. It's all energy!!

2. Journaling

Write down anything you can do or let go of to clean up your money energy. You can also look at any other areas of your life you feel called to clean up today.

1. _____

2. _____

3. _____

4. _____

5. _____

6. _____

7. _____

8. _____

9. _____

10. _____

After you've released and cleaned up any money leaks, make sure to celebrate that you've patched up the energy leaks tied to your finances. Bringing in a lot of love and appreciation for your money is key to attracting more!

Whooo hoooo to you and elevating your abundance levels...no matter where you are financially, we can all bring more love into this area of our life. This will infuse more elevated energy into our finances and will allow us to attract more!

We need more abundant, elevated people in the world, and you deserve to be fully supported and able to give back to great causes in big ways!!

If you have any limiting beliefs around money, just know you can easily move through those blocks.

Bonus Challenge: Here is a great mantra to play on low when you sleep or when you work: Aap Sahaee Hoa (Meditation for Prosperity). You can find it on the Mantras for Prosperity album by Spirit Voyage or on our Spotify Playlist in the 21-Day Challenge Tool Kit.

Here are some great conscious mindset affirmation tools. Say these 3-5 times, 3-5 times a day.

I am a magnet for money. Prosperity is drawn to me.

Money comes to me in expected and unexpected ways.

I move from poverty thinking to abundance thinking.

I am worthy of making more money.

*I am open and receptive to all the wealth life offers me.**

movement

DAY 13: Move Your Bod

You didn't think we were going to spend this whole challenge chilling on the couch, did you? Hell no! All this reflection and journaling has been super valuable, but it's time to shake things up a little.

Today, we're starting to focus on movement, which is a powerful tool to move energy and lift your vibrational frequency.

As you're well aware by now, you are made of energy. In order to raise your vibration, rise up the emotional scale, and evolve, your energy has to be able to circulate freely. But here's the thing: Just like the drains in your house sometimes run a little slow, your energy flow can also get stuck sometimes. If you don't tap into stagnant energy in your body, you remain stagnant in your overall life. Whether you're feeling held back by limiting thoughts, an unfulfilling job, or a dead-end relationship, it doesn't matter — without generating new energy in the body and busting through the blocks (AKA slow energy flow in the body), you'll stay stuck in the same place you are now.

The GOD Cycle

According to Yogi Bhajan (and many other scientists and philosophers), energy works in a circular motion. We'll go into more of this later, but for now, just know that all energy Generates, Organizes, and Destroys. GOD. We are born, we live, and we die. We eat, digest, and eliminate. Everything works this way.

If you don't generate energy in the body… if you don't organize and pay attention to where that energy is going…and if you don't exert energy or let it go … you won't be able to raise the vibration of your energy or achieve more elevated emotions. One really efficient way to do *all* of these things? Movement. (Kundalini yoga, specifically!)

No matter how young or old you are, you need to be moving consciously every day — generating energy, directing it where it's needed, and letting go of stagnant energy — to elevate even more.

TODAY'S CHALLENGE

Do some conscious movement. Today, we're going to start with an easy, but super effective form of movement: CAT-COW.

There are many different postures in Kundalini yoga, but cat-cow, specifically, is a full kriya, meaning a full set of postures, in just one movement. It's a great way to move energy quickly through your body, and it loosens, adjusts, and increases the flexibility of the spine.

The flexibility of the spine was a topic that Yogi Bhajan often talked about as being overlooked, but it's incredibly important to living a life of vitality. The spinal cord is responsible for keeping us upright and relaying signals to the brain that control our movement and organ function. Yogi Bhajan said, "The flexible spine holds your entire nervous system." And like we've talked about, to hold more high-vibrational energy in our bodies, our nervous systems need to be strong enough to handle and sustain it. So we can give the body a vitality boost by giving the spine an excellent stretch and workout with just three minutes of cat-cow - it's that easy!

Here's how it's done:

1. Begin on your hands and knees with your hands underneath your shoulders, fingers facing forward and spread out wide, and your knees directly under your hips.

2. Inhale, expanding your stomach out. At the same time, tilt your pelvis forward and down. Arch your back, raising and stretching your chin up and back (cow position), opening your heart as wide as you can without scrunching your neck.

3. Exhale and tilt the pelvis in the opposite direction, arching the spine up towards the sky (cat position), bringing the chin into the chest.

4. Continue this movement slowly, and as your body warms up, begin to move at a more rapid pace. Set a timer for 3 minutes.

5. To End: Inhale deeply and hold cow position, stretching your heart open. Then exhale, arching your spine up to the sky and bringing your chin into your chest. Push back into child's pose with your forehead on the ground, and your hands stretched out in front of you in prayer pose. This will balance the hemispheres of the brain.

If you want more Kundalini yoga, you can also choose to join us in our 528 Academy, where we have a whole library of Kundalini yoga classes, meditations, and kriyas. Visit www.elevatetheglobe.com to sign up!

Bonus Challenge: We sometimes forget about what a perfect exercise walking is — especially those of us who live in cities where we drive everywhere! But our bodies are made to walk, and we should be trying to fit it in whenever we can.

Download the Stepz app or look at the Health app on your iPhone and start becoming aware of how much you walk. Today, create a goal for yourself — maybe 5,000 or 10,000 steps — and look for ways to walk more! With time, you can build up to 15,000 steps.

Yogi Bhajan advised women to walk 4-6 miles a day (1-3 miles is a good start in today's commuting culture), especially women preparing to have a child, during pregnancy, and after the child is born. We swing both arms as we walk which clears our aura, according to Yogi Bhajan. This is especially key for people already walking 5,000-10,000 steps a day to bump it up a notch! So put your headphones on, play some mantras, put your phone in your pocket, and let your arms be FREE as you move your body and clear your aura!

Ever since we started to become more conscious about walking more, we challenge ourselves to make sure we're walking enough each day. It seems so simple, but we've definitely noticed that we have so much more energy and endurance!

Holy, moving your body!! You are more than halfway through the challenge. This is the time to really finish strong. See you tomorrow to talk about high vibrational nutrition!

nutrition

DAY 14: Eat Intuitively

We're coming back to all things nutrition today! You might be surprised that food is such a big part of this challenge, but it's intimately connected with high-vibrational living.

As we talked about before, food carries a unique vibration. And if you're working so hard to raise yours, don't you want to eat only the foods that help you maintain a blissful, loving state? When you start to look at food on the vibrational scale, you'll notice that plants carry the highest energetic frequencies. It can really blow your mind and change the way you look at food. Check out the graphic below, it's super cool!

*High vs. Low Vibrational Foods**

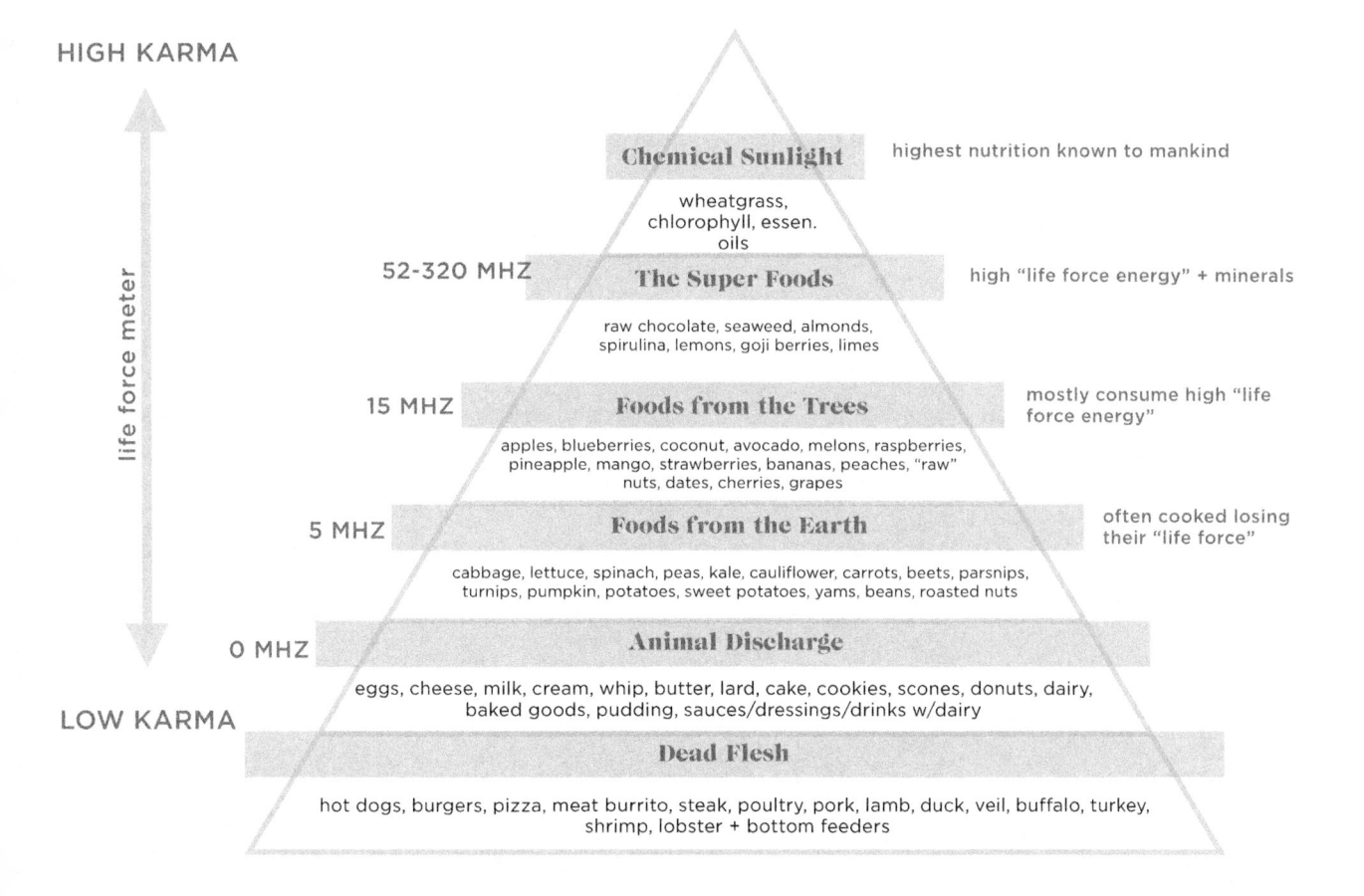

HIGH KARMA

life force meter

Chemical Sunlight — highest nutrition known to mankind

wheatgrass, chlorophyll, essen. oils

52-320 MHZ — **The Super Foods** — high "life force energy" + minerals

raw chocolate, seaweed, almonds, spirulina, lemons, goji berries, limes

15 MHZ — **Foods from the Trees** — mostly consume high "life force energy"

apples, blueberries, coconut, avocado, melons, raspberries, pineapple, mango, strawberries, bananas, peaches, "raw" nuts, dates, cherries, grapes

5 MHZ — **Foods from the Earth** — often cooked losing their "life force"

cabbage, lettuce, spinach, peas, kale, cauliflower, carrots, beets, parsnips, turnips, pumpkin, potatoes, sweet potatoes, yams, beans, roasted nuts

0 MHZ — **Animal Discharge**

eggs, cheese, milk, cream, whip, butter, lard, cake, cookies, scones, donuts, dairy, baked goods, pudding, sauces/dressings/drinks w/dairy

LOW KARMA

Dead Flesh

hot dogs, burgers, pizza, meat burrito, steak, poultry, pork, lamb, duck, veil, buffalo, turkey, shrimp, lobster + bottom feeders

High water content foods have a higher vibration than low water content foods

Wild foods have a higher vibration than domesticated/cultivated/hybridized/GMO Foods

Organic foods have a higher vibration than conventionally grown foods (with use of pesticides, herbicides, fungicides, larvicides, etc. which are all toxic poisons)

Raw foods have a higher vibration than cooked foods. The longer the cooking time and the higher the temperature, the lower the vibration. (Lightly steamed is better than boiled, which is better than baked, which is better than fried, which is the worst.)

Fresh foods have a higher vibration than packaged foods (such as grapes vs. raisins)

Whole foods have a higher vibration than processed foods (such as quinoa vs. white bread)

Vegan foods (such as fruits, vegetables, nuts, seeds, legumes, and grains) have a higher vibration than flesh/animal foods (such as meat, fish, eggs, and dairy)

Lighter foods have a higher vibration than heavier/denser foods (such as fruits vs nuts)

But remember, no matter what the vibrational scale may say, we are all different and react to food in our own unique way. Because of this, it's your job to find out what jives well with your body and what doesn't, so that you're eating to feel your best. Some plant-based foods might not agree with you, and that's okay. When you tune into the vibration of the food and your body, you become aware of what eating to feel your best means to you.

"I found out I had a slight allergy and sensitivity to wheat, which was a huge bummer because it meant I had to learn a new way of eating, but I was up for the challenge because I was up for feeling my most energetic, clearest, and happiest self. I began to take it out of my diet slowly and noticed that I didn't get bloated, emotional, or tired after eating anymore (must have been eating a lot of wheat!) and this change has completely given me more control over my emotional state, my body weight, and my mind." - **Tara**

It's all about awareness!

Green Zoodles
ZUCCHINI NOODLES W/ AVOCADO SAUCE

YOU WILL NEED
- 1 zucchini
- 1/3 cup water (85 ml)
- 2 tbsp lemon juice
- 1 avocado
- 4 tbsp pine nuts
- 1 1/4 cup holy basil (30 g)
- 12 cherry tomatoes

PROCEDURE
- Make the zucchini noodles using a peeler or a spiralizer
- Blend the rest of the ingredients (except the cherry tomatoes) in a blender until smooth
- In a large bowl, combine noodles, avocado sauce and cherry tomatoes
- Substitution Ideas: broccoli or squash instead of zucchini

High Vibe Detox
PINEAPPLE TURMERIC GINGER SMOOTHIE

YOU WILL NEED
- 1 cup pineapple
- 2 naval oranges, quartered and peeled
- 1-inch piece of ginger, peeled
- 1/2 inch piece of turmeric, peeled (or 1 tsp powdered turmeric)
- a pinch of black pepper + sea salt
- 1 cup almond milk
- 2 tsp almond or sesame oil

PROCEDURE
- Mix all of the ingredients and blend well, until smooth
- Pour and serve
- Substitution Ideas: mango or peach instead of pineapple

TODAY'S CHALLENGE

Make the noodles or smoothie recipe on the previous page, or eat one balanced plant-based/vegan meal today of your choice.

After each meal and snack, write down what you ate in the Food Log below, and note how you felt afterward. Use the following questions as guidance.*

1. Do you feel awake, with enhanced energy?
2. Do you feel tired after eating?
3. Do you have any bloating or gas?
4. Any pain or stiffness of joints?
5. How is your sleep? Better, worse, or the same?
6. Do you have brain fog or do you feel alert and sharp?

DATE:
BREAKFAST:
HOW I FELT:

SNACK (IF ANY):
HOW I FELT:

LUNCH:
HOW I FELT:

SNACK (IF ANY):
HOW I FELT:

DINNER:
HOW I FELT:

END WITH A SUMMARY OF TODAY'S EATING EXPERIENCE:

Do this for as many days as needed to get a good handle on what your body feels best eating.

ETG TIP: If you have digestive issues, Yogi Bhajan said to eat an apple after your meal. We also love eating a little papaya or taking a papaya enzyme supplement which helps with digestion.

Bonus Challenge: Depending on where you are in your nutrition journey, you may or may not feel like you need to change what you eat. If you do, don't stress — you're in the majority.

We suggest focusing on adding things into your diet, versus taking things out. We find people really struggle with forcing themselves to cut out dairy, sugar, or processed foods if they aren't ready. So it's often easier to add in healthier and more high-vibrational foods and then see what you end up not wanting anymore. You'll probably be surprised!

Try adding a few extra fruits and vegetables to one of your meals today. Notice whether this helps curb your cravings for less-than-healthy food throughout the day.

It's our little trick on our mind and taste buds. If we fill up on the good stuff, we'll have less room in our stomachs for the bad stuff!

"I used to never think I would be able to stop eating cheese —literally, the pizza guy knew us because he came at least once a week. It was a part of our family culture. But when I started adding in more superfoods and making my own vegan recipes, I realized I didn't have to deprive myself, but just make shifts. I grew to love smoothies, Buddha bowls, vegan Caesar salads, vegan pizza, and other healthier things that made me feel good. And I lost the pizza delivery place's number and started dialing into my vitality and optimal health." - Britt

connection

DAY 15: Give Yourself All of the Love

The phrase "self-care" gets thrown around a lot in the wellness world today. But to us, the concept is about so much more than just taking a selfie in front of Netflix with a #selfcaresunday hashtag. Every day, we find a little time to do ancient, conscious self-care practices that can raise our vibration to a whole new level!

We have studied for years with yogi masters who trained with Yogi Bhajan, who brought Kundalini yoga and meditation from India to the west. We have learned so much about how to properly care for our bodies and minds from a yogic perspective, and are super passionate about passing on these gems to our community.

Why? Well, there is a lot of energy in the collective consciousness making us think that it's selfish to care for ourselves first. We feel the exact opposite. In our experience, giving to ourselves first is the only way we have the energy to actually express our true selves, give, and uplift others. The best analogy is that, on an airplane, they tell you to put your oxygen mask on first before helping your children. If you don't have enough oxygen and pass out, then you and the child will both go down — feel us? And we want everyone elevating on the planet, don't you? So this is how we do it.

We give ourselves some badass, unapologetic self-love and care.

We expect it, and we create boundaries to allow it into our lives.

Then, we feel good and can show up for ourselves, our families, our friends, and everyone we meet with a shit-ton of light and love. Think Care-Bears-shooting-light-out-of-their-stomachs vibes.

TODAY'S CHALLENGE

**Find 15 minutes in your schedule for some self-care.
Answer the journal prompt after your experience.**

Maybe it's an Epsom salt bath, a face mask, or some time alone. Perhaps it's making a beautiful meal or taking 15 minutes to play mantras and sit in silence and feel yourself in your own body.

We have so many ancient yogic self-care practices that are entirely life-changing, so we wanted to share two of our favorites from our 8-week course, RISE UP: A Chakra Course in High Vibrational Living — cold showers (hydrotherapy) and the Divine Feminine Bath Ritual.

We encourage you to try one or both for today's challenge as these are both important self-care elements in this yogic lifestyle and have so many amazing benefits…the cold shower is not that bad, promise!

Rise Up Bath
DIVINE FEMININE BATH RITUAL

Bathing rituals are a great way to release our daily routines, connect with our divine feminine energy (yin) and balance our our masculine energy (yang). The Divine Mother is within all of us. She's a protector, she's compassionate, powerful, sharp, graceful, naturing, and creative. She is YOU.

HOW TO DO IT

- **Minerals:** Himalayan Sea Salt + Epsom Salt
- **Flowers/Herbs/Oils:** Rose, Ylang Ylang, Gardenia, Lavender, Rosemary (use a tea leaf strainer for those smaller herbs/flowers)
- **Crystals:** Rose Quartz (unconditional love), Citrine (creativity + abundance)
- **Listen to the Adi Shakti Mantra** while you're bathing. The Adi Shakti Mantra tunes one into the frequency of the Divine Mother, and to the primal protective, generating energy. You can find this mantra on YouTube.

Adi Shakti, Adi Shakti, Namo Namo (I bow to the Primal Power)
Sarb Shakti, Sarb Shakti, Sarb Shakti, Namo Namo (I bow to the all encompassing Power + Energy)
Pritham Bhagvati, Pritham Bhagvati, Pritham Bhagvati, Namo Namo (I bow to that which God creates)
Kundalini Mata Shakti, Mata Shakti, Namo Namo (I bow to the creative power of the Kundalini, the Divine Mother Power)

Cold Showers
AS TAUGHT BY YOGI BHAJAN

Yogi Bhajan taught that cold water stimulates the blood in the internal organs, it cleanses and energizes the glandular system, and gives us the grit to meet the challenges we face. He also taught that especially for women, cold showers help her maintain her glow. It's recommended to practice taking a cold shower once per week and always precede with a massage of almond oil or olive oil.

BENEFITS OF A COLD SHOWER PER YOGI BHAJAN

- **brings blood** to the capillaries
- **cleans** the circulatory system
- **reduces blood pressure** on internal organs, flushing internal organs and giving them a new supply of blood
- **strengthens** the parasympathetic and sympathetic nervous systems
- **contracts** the muscles and causes them to **eliminate toxins and poisons** more quickly
- brings **the power of resistance and resilience** to the body
- **strengthens** the mucous membranes
- keeps the **skin young and shining**
- **prevents** the body from developing an extra layer of fat, which affects the liver
- **balances** the glands
- circulation and nerve **problems can be prevented** by regular cold showers

What is your relationship to self-care after you spent 15 minutes on yourself today? How do you feel now vs. before? Did any emotions come up that surprised you or that you want to note?

_____

_____

_____

_____

Ok, now you are glowing from the inside out! We are really about to elevate big time ... see you tomorrow!

DAY 16: Listen to Signs from the Universe

Now that you're giving back to yourself and have your metaphorical oxygen mask on, we need you to wake up and PAY ATTENTION. To what, you ask? To the universe. This world we are living in. What is it telling you?

We get messages all day, every day to guide us in the right direction. Source, God, the universe, angels, energy, love — whatever you want to call this energy, it's up to you — talks to us. It communicates through signs, numbers, synchronicities, and messages.

Angels and this universal energy of love are all around us and available to connect with! Depending on where you are on your spiritual journey, you may have connected with them consciously (or not), but it's never too late to start. All you have to do is be open and willing. They are made of light, and they can guide us in different ways, in different areas of our life.

But a lot of the time, people are so busy that they don't notice these divine nudges — or they're not aware that they're experiencing a sign from the universe, and so they pass it off as a coincidence. You may be totally aware and work with signs, but no matter where you are in your journey, you can always elevate higher and up your connection. So let's do it!!

How does the universe speak to us?

There are many different signs the universe can deliver showing us that it's got our back. Here are some common ones to look out for:

- **Feathers:** If you come across a lot of feathers or see them in your spaces, it's a sign that the angelic realm is near and you're on track. Continue to deepen your connection to the spiritual realms.
- **Fragrance:** These are sometimes unidentifiable scents, but they can also be floral, sweet, or remind you of a loved one who passed.
- **Babies and Pets:** Our little ones are very much in tune with the angelic presence and energy around us. So if you notice a baby staring off into the distance or pointing — especially at the ceiling — or your dog starts barking at random areas, this is a big sign that angels are nearby!

- **Music:** People have reported hearing angelic sounds and or angels signing from somewhere not in the physical surroundings.
- **Coins:** Finding coins is a sign that the divine is giving you gifts and abundance. It's a message that the universe is supporting you.
- **Numbers:** Angel numbers are one of the most common signs, and they are easy to recognize. If you see a certain number or sequence of numbers a lot, consider it to be a personal message for you. The more you pay attention and not take them for granted or ignore them, the more you will know them.
- **Voices:** If you hear a voice or someone calling out your name — and no one is there physically — it's a way of the angels getting your attention and showing you are protected.
- **Words/Messages/Advertisements:** Messages can come through everything you see. You might see a particular word or shape or color in different ways, and it may convey messages to you. Again, this is a way that the universe directs your attention to things that can help guide you.
- **Feelings:** Our sixth sense is very sharp and a powerful tool to not be underestimated. If you ever get the chills or other physical sensations, they may be divine help — nothing to be scared of!

Deepening your connection with the universe.

As you become more and more spiritually aware — especially through Kundalini yoga and meditation — you will start to connect more and more and receive guidance. There is so much to learn about the Archangels and so many angels to connect with, and it's such a fun journey to deepen this connection.

We always tap into divine energy and angels at the beginning of our day, especially to listen to any direction or guidance we should follow.

We use this prayer from A Course in Miracles to help with this connection:

What would You have me do?

Where would You have me go?

What would You have me say, and to whom?

TODAY'S CHALLENGE

Ask the universe to give you a sign for a specific area of your life.

You can choose a specific sign, or ask to be shown a sign. Write down what you're asking for below and start to pay attention to all the ways the universe and the angels are talking to you. And this is important — trust that it will show up in the way it's supposed to.

"I remember the first sign I asked for was about a specific romantic relationship. I asked out loud to be shown a sign, and the first thing that came to my mind was...a goose. I thought that was really an odd thing. Not, like, a butterfly or unicorn or some beautiful thing...a goose. Really? But I trusted my internal voice and said, 'Okay if this is what you want me to work with, show it to me in physical form.' I started seeing videos of geese on Instagram, on physical road signs on the highway, and actual geese in lakes and out in nature. They were everywhere! It wasn't until later that I stumbled upon the symbolism of the goose — it mates for life with its partner. That's when I felt, 'WOW, of course, that was my sign for this relationship question.' I felt like my guides and angels were delivering another message to trust that when you hear something after you've asked for it, that's the answer, even if it seems weird." - Tara

So now it's time, ask for your sign!

_____

_____

_____

_____

DAY 17: Get to Know Your Astrological Birth Chart

We couldn't be more excited about today! Astrology is Tara's favorite topic ever, and we both use the stars to guide our meditations and the monthly content in our 528 Academy. When you pair astrology with Kundalini yoga — and the high levels of awareness and intuition it activates — it truly gives you superpowers.

Plus, one of the most essential acts of self-love you can practice is to learn more about yourself and learn to be in harmony with your own energetic blueprint — AKA your astrological birth chart.

Put simply, astrology is the study of the movements and positions of the planets, which are thought to have an influence on us and the natural world. Most importantly, astrology is a tool we can use to be in harmony with our planet at all times, allowing us to consciously work with the energy available to us.

Your horoscope isn't the only astrological tool you should know about. It's also really fun to learn about your **birth chart. The** birth chart is basically a blueprint of where all the planets were when you were born, and it's calculated by using your birth date, birth time, and birthplace. (You can calculate your birth chart for free at https://alabe.com/freechart/)

Among the coolest things in your birth chart are the two specific points that hold information about your destiny and life lessons. These are known as the north node and the south node — or, collectively, "the lunar nodes."

The lunar nodes are directly opposite each other in your chart. They aren't planets, but two mathematical locations. The north node represents what we've come here to learn, what we're aiming to embody and master in this lifetime. The south node reveals our gifts, our challenges, our comfort zones, and what we need to let go of in this lifetime.

By just investigating this part of our charts, we can learn so much about ourselves — what our soul is yearning to learn and what it would like to release. And when we're living in harmony with this, it will help keep us in those high-vibrational emotions we're aiming for.

TODAY'S CHALLENGE

Find your birthday on this chart to discover your north node and south node. Then, read on to discover what they hold in store for you regarding what to release and what to embrace in this lifetime.

NORTH + SOUTH NODE DATES (1941-2034)

South Node/North Node	Release	Embrace
Aries South Node/ Libra North Node Jun 17, 1958 — Dec 15, 1959 Jan 8, 1977 — Jul 5, 1978 Aug 1, 1995 — Jan 25 1997 Feb 19, 2014 — Nov 11, 2015 Oct 15, 2032 — May 22, 2034	Too much self-reliance Excessive competitiveness Rushing into things	Tact/cooperation with others Putting yourself in another's shoes Patience
Taurus South Node/ Scorpio North Node Oct 5, 1956 — Jun 16, 1958 Jul 10, 1975 — Jan 7, 1977 Feb 2, 1994 — Jul 31, 1995 Aug 30, 2012 — Feb 18, 2014 Mar 21, 2031 — Oct 14, 2032	Attachment to luxury and material possessions Being too set in your ways Being overly focused on security	Simplicity in your possessions Spiritual fulfillment Embracing change and the mystery of life
Gemini South Node/ Sagittarius North Node Apr 3, 1955 — Oct 4, 1956 Oct 28, 1973 — July 9, 1975 Aug 2, 1992 — Feb 1, 1994 Mar 4, 2011 — Aug 29, 2012 Sept 24, 2029 — Mar 20, 2031	Gossip Information overload that leaves you unable to make decisions Scattering your energy in too many directions	The big picture Leaving your comfort zone and taking risks Higher learning, travel and adventure
Cancer South Node/ Capricorn North Node Oct 10, 1953 — Apr 2, 1955 Apr 28, 1972 — Oct 27, 1973 Nov 19, 1990 — Aug 1, 1992 Aug 22, 2009 — Mar 3, 2011 March 27, 2028 — Sept 23, 2029	Caretaking/enabling Being too dependent on others Overly emotional responses and attachment to childhood	Leadership in public/private life Developing discipline and professional skills Empowering others

South Node/North Node	Release	Embrace
Leo South Node/ Aquarius North Node Mar 29, 1952 — Oct 9, 1953 Nov 3, 1970 — Apr 27, 1972 May 23, 1989 — Nov 18, 1990 Dec 19, 2007 — Aug 21, 2009 July 27, 2026 — Mar 26, 2028	Over-the-top attention-seeking Attraction to drama and making it all about you Taking things personally	A team spirit and appreciating others for their uniqueness Freedom that comes from a sense of purpose "We are all equal"
Virgo South Node/ Pisces North Node Jul 27, 1950 — Mar 28, 1952 Apr 20, 1969 — Nov 2, 1970 Dec 3, 1987 — May 22, 1989 Jun 23, 2006 — Dec 18, 2007 Jan 12, 2025 — July 26, 2026	Perfectionism Doing things by yourself or the hard way Controlling, overanalyzing, worrying	Being the healer Tapping into your creativity and developing your imagination Surrendering to and trusting your psychic abilities
Libra South Node/ Aries North Node Jan 27, 1949 — Jul 26, 1950 Aug 20, 1967 — Apr 19, 1969 Apr 7, 1986 — Dec 2, 1987 Dec 27, 2004 — Jun 22, 2006 Jul 18, 2023 — Jan 11, 2025	Codependency in one-to-one relationships Indecisiveness Being the peacekeeper	Stepping out as a leader Loving yourself deeply Acting on your impulses
Scorpio South Node/ Taurus North Node Aug 3, 1947 — Jan 26, 1949 Feb 20, 1966 — Aug 19, 1967 Sep 12, 1984 — Apr 6, 1986 Apr 15, 2003 — Dec 26, 2004 Jan 19, 2022 — July 17, 2023	Seducing, manipulating, secrecy, and need to create crisis The nomadic lifestyle Defining your worth and values by your significant others	Grounding, daily habits Living in the present moment Rolling up your sleeves and getting to work
Sagittarius South Node/ Gemini North Node Dec 14, 1945 — Aug 2, 1947 Aug 26, 1964 — Feb 19, 1966 Mar 17, 1983 — Sep 11, 1984 Oct 14, 2001 — Apr 14, 2003 May 6, 2020 — Jan 18, 2022	Ungrounded wanderlust Rushing through life Fearing freedom will be taken from you if you slow down	Listening to others and refining social graces Playful exploration Partnerships without the fear of being tied down

South Node/North Node	Release	Embrace
Capricorn South Node/ Cancer North Node May 12, 1944 — Dec 3, 1945 Dec 24, 1962 — Aug 25, 1964 Sep 25, 1981 — Mar 16, 1983 Apr 10, 2000 — Oct 13, 2001 Nov 7, 2018 — May 5, 2020	The need to be in control Being a workaholic and an elitist Fear of depending on others	Emotional sensitivity Making time for your "home base" and family life Following intuition first to feed your ambition
Aquarius South Node/ Leo North Node Nov 22, 1942 — May 11, 1944 Jun 11, 1961 — Dec 23, 1962 Jan 6, 1980 — Sep 24, 1981 Oct 21, 1998 — Apr 10, 2000 May 10, 2017 — Nov 6, 2018	Worrying about what people think Hiding out in groups and being afraid to stand out as an individual Being emotionally detached and impersonal	Sharing your creative self-expression without fear Taking personal risks and leading by example Following your heart
Pisces South Node/ Virgo North Node May 25, 1941 — Nov 21, 1942 Dec 16, 1959 — Jun 10, 1961 Jul 6, 1978 — Jan 5, 1980 Jan 26, 1997 — Oct 20, 1998 Nov 12, 2015 — May 9, 2017	Emotional manipulation, self-pity, and excuses Scattered, nomadic living Getting lost in daydreams and fantasies	Solving problems with systems and facts Developing structure and daily routines in your life Paying attention to details and organization

Remember we are all made of stardust and you are shining bright!! We'll talk about tantric numerology tomorrow. Keep your commitment game strong, your future self is thanking you already!!

DAY 18: Calculate Your Tantric Numerology

You may have heard about numerology, which is the universal language of numbers and the study of their meanings and personalities. Trust us, this is way more fun than what you learned in math class: Like astrology, numerology is an insanely fascinating tool to help us understand our strengths and weaknesses. It can help us decode our unique patterns and life purpose, and demystify the world around us.

In the Kundalini yoga tradition, we use tantric numerology, which is a little different from traditional numerology. In this system, the language of numbers is understood through the yogic ten bodies and the number eleven. In yogic philosophy, a human is made up of ten bodies: the physical body, three mental bodies, and six energy bodies. The eleventh embodiment is when you have all of your ten bodies under your command, and you're able to consciously access all the parts of yourself. If you don't know what the ten bodies are, check them out here.

1st - Soul Body

2nd - Negative Mind

3rd - Positive Mind

4th - Neutral Mind

5th - Physical Body

6th - Arcline

7th - Aura

8th - Pranic Body

9th - Subtle Body

10th - Radiant Body

When we use tantric numerology and apply it to our lives, we strengthen each of our ten bodies and learn how to master ourselves — and that helps keep us in a high-vibe emotional state.

TODAY'S CHALLENGE

Head over to https://www.3ho.org/3ho-lifestyle/tantric-numerology/reading to get a personal Tantric Numerology Reading.

Then, take time to journal about what stood out to you in your reading. What can you use from this insight to enhance and elevate your life?

___

___

___

___

___

___

___

___

___

___

Want to learn more? Our great friend Remington Donovan is a tantric numerologist, and we had him on our podcast, The Elevator. Check out episode 19 — Tantric Numerology + Elevating Your Growth — to dive deeper into this topic!

manifesting

DAY 19: Become Immensely Grateful

It's been so fun getting to know our birth charts and tantric numerology, right? Well, another major component to elevating higher and manifesting a life you love is coming back down to earth and experiencing GRATITUDE.

As you're co-creating with your higher self/the universe/God/whatever you want to call it — feeling better and upgrading your life in the process — it's important to appreciate your current state. This isn't about staying stagnant or content with the status quo. But to keep evolving, growing, and loving yourself and your life more and more, the key is to always stay immensely grateful for where you are right now.

"Life moves pretty fast. If you don't stop and look around once in a while, you could miss it." -Ferris Bueller (LOL, gotta always have the humor!)

There are so many studies showing that people who regularly practice gratitude experience more positive emotions, feel more alive, sleep better, express more compassion and kindness, and even have stronger immune systems.* So even though it may feel hard to be grateful for anything when you're in the midst of, like, a breakup or an illness, this practice can actually help you get through those hard times.

There's always something to be grateful for.

How do we become immensely grateful? First, we have to tap into actually feeling our blessings on all levels and understand how much we honestly have to be grateful for.

Putting things into perspective: Half of the world's population (more than 3 billion people) lives on less than $2.50 a day. More than 1.3 billion live in extreme poverty — less than $1.25 a day. 805 million people don't have enough food to eat, and according to UNICEF, 22,000 children die each day due to poverty.

That can bring up some sadness, but we say this to make you realize how insanely blessed we all are to have been able to buy this workbook, to be ALIVE and reading it, to have food to eat, and legs to walk with.

If we ever forget all we have to be grateful for, we can end up focusing on what we *don't* have. This is bad news — it sends us sliding down the emotional spiral, fast. But finding gratitude for the little things helps us rise back up towards those high-vibration emotions that act as a magnet for our wildest dreams. Just ask Oprah:

"Being grateful all the time isn't easy. But it's when you least feel thankful that you are most in need of what gratitude can give you: perspective. Gratitude can transform any situation. It alters your vibration, moving you from negative energy to positive. It's the quickest, easiest, most powerful way to effect change in your life — this I know for sure."
-Oprah Winfrey

When you start on Oprah quotes, it's hard to stop so we had to do one more...

"I started out giving thanks for the small things, and the more thankful I became, the more my bounty increased. That's because — for sure — what you focus on expands. When you focus on the goodness in your life, you create more of it." - **Oprah Winfrey**

We've experienced the amazing ways that gratitude can shift our energy, and we're sure you have too. But we can always take it up a notch. The more you make gratitude a part of your every day — especially at the beginning of your day — the more you'll notice the change it sparks.

"When my Mom was diagnosed with stage 4 lung cancer, I realized, if I was really honest with myself, I took A LOT for granted. At the time, I took for granted that I felt good and was well, that could get up and drive to work, eat great food, brush my teeth on my own, that I had the freedom to do what I wanted. All that was taken away from my Mom in a flash, and it made me realize all of these things I complained about having to do were gifts. From there, in that new place of actually feeling gratitude, a lot in my life shifted." - Britt

So how can we most effectively practice gratitude?

Like everything, you have to find what works best for your lifestyle and your energy. But we've studied and practiced a lot of the techniques out there, and we have some great tips that'll help you cultivate a massive pot of gratitude at the end of your daily rainbow.

Research* by UC Davis psychologist Robert Emmons, author of *Thanks!: How the New Science of Gratitude Can Make You Happier*, shows that merely keeping a gratitude journal — regularly writing down moments that make you feel thankful — can significantly increase well-being and life satisfaction.

To supercharge this whole gratitude thing, we practice it in our Magic Morning Ritual, which we share in our course RISE UP. After we tune in and do a little breathwork (Ego Eradicator with breath of fire!), we think of or write down 3-5 things we are thankful for. It instantly lifts our vibration and starts the day in such high and great energy!

Already doing this? Here are some tips to take your gratitude practice to the next level.

1. Be grateful for the "good" and "bad": The ultimate test of your gratitude practice is finding the silver lining in *everything*. Ask yourself, "Why and how is this happening FOR ME? What can I be grateful for in this challenging moment or situation?"

2. Be mindful about gratitude: Make it a practice to think about what you are grateful for as much as possible — not just after meditation. If you find yourself in a self-destructive thought pattern during the day, start to think about all the wonderful things in your life that you can be grateful for. The key here is to actually visualize it and feel it in your body.

3. Share your gratitude: We totally get that these kinds of things can feel really personal. But if you want to up your gratitude game, tell someone else what you're grateful for! Share how much you appreciate those around you, and it will help you in badass ways. Soul Pancake, a company that researches the "science of happiness," did an experiment where they asked people to write a letter to a person they were grateful for. That alone increased their happiness levels by 2%. Then, when those same people made a phone call to the person they were thankful for, to express their gratitude directly, happiness levels went up 15%. It's so cool to us that science is able to prove this stuff now!

TODAY'S CHALLENGE

Start a gratitude journal!
At least for today, write down 3-5 things you are grateful for below.

You can do it in the beginning or at the end of your day, and feel free to keep it going every day in a specific gratitude journal. No idea is too small — even if it's a little thing like being thankful for your fingers so you can write this list. Feel the gratitude and visualize it if you can.

1. _____

2. _____

3. _____

4. _____

5. _____

Bonus Challenge: To take this a step further, text or call someone and TELL them how grateful you are for them! Let us know how this goes in the FB group or on Instagram @elevatetheglobe!

Gratitude game strong. Two days left ... whattt?! You're so close to the finish line! Tomorrow we are manifesting...can't wait to see you there.

DAY 20: Manifest + Visualize Your Dream Life

WOW — we can't believe we only have two more days of this challenge! (We can assure you they're going to be good ones.) Can we just take a minute to say how happy we are for you? Celebrate how far you've come, no matter what that looks like, and make it part of your gratitude and self-love practice for today.

Yesterday was BIG-time priming you for today. We're about to give you some tools to set up the rest of your year (and life!) for more happiness, health, and high vibes.

Manifesting is such a fun topic — Britt's fav! — and it's basically a process for attracting all of the things you want. All the work we've done so far has been preparing you to be a master manifestor. Are you ready?

"Manifesting and optimism were the main topics that really sparked my spiritual journey as a child. I was always really drawn to inspirational stories that widened my belief in what was possible.

When I was around 11, I used to love to do ceremonies, and I would get all my friends to light candles and write down what we wanted and then bury it in the backyard in a box. I would read Chicken Soup for the Teenage Soul all the time. Then, my uncle got me The Secret because one of his friends was featured in the book and movie, and I thought that was the coolest thing in the world. I then watched The Secret movie, and I would always practice doing magic and manifesting and started deeply connecting to the universe! I couldn't imagine not working with the Law of Attraction and tapping into this wisdom and way of living.

It continues to be something I love to learn about and teach, and it has allowed me to manifest a beautiful reality." - Britt

There's so much we could go into here — and we dive into manifesting in a big way in our eight-week course, RISE UP — but we wanted to give you some essential tips to start manifesting everything on your vision board right NOW!

Bottom line: Like everything else, it's all about being in a high vibrational state. When you're in elevated energy — and not sitting in the low vibes of shame, jealousy, comparison, etc. — you can attract things that are of the highest good for your soul, rather than desiring things to feel worthy. Trying to find happiness in outside things never works, because what's still there when you get that thing? YOU.

You are always the constant in anything you do, and when you're unhappy inside, nothing else outside of you will "fix it". But when you go within and connect to your true self and your true desires — you know, everything we've been working on over the past 19 days! — you create happiness within and everything changes. It's from here that you can create the life of your dreams. You become aligned with your divine soul mission, and you can fulfill your purpose for being on this planet.

Yogi Bhajan always said "happiness is your birthright," and we live by this every day. We use meditation, breathwork, self-love, and more to feel full within ourselves first. And because of this, we believe we are worthy of anything we want — like peace, joy, cool cars, high levels of health, homes by the beach, texts from friends, and lunches at Rose Cafe in Venice.

So you might be thinking "This sounds great and all, but how the F#@K do I do it?!" We're breaking it down for you here. We have created what we believe to be the most effective way to manifest anything you desire, informed by all the books, workshops, documentaries, and trainings we've experienced over the years. (And our own practices with manifesting, of course.)

If you've been manifesting for years, we think this breakdown will really help you take things to the next level!

Elevate The Globe's 7 Manifesting Steps

1. **Ask with clarity:** Become clear and specific about what you want (meditation helps so much with this!) and ask for it from the universe. Know the "why" behind your desire and be authentic with yourself about how this will bring you happiness and elevate your soul. You only need to ask and declare to the universe once. In doing so, you allow yourself to move away from the "want" stage.

2. **Feel + visualize it:** Feel the emotion and the energy of your desire as if it's already manifested. Act as if it's already happened. How will you act when this happens? Who would you be? We practice visualization every morning after our meditation. We also love using vision boards, images, and real-life examples of what we want to manifest. Our subconscious mind works in imagery, so seeing it in our minds allows us to experience our desire and be on its vibrational frequency so we can magnetize it to us.

3. **Take action:** The universe will guide you to your desire, but you must show up and do the work along the way to getting there. Kundalini yoga is an excellent tool for generating more life force energy that will help you practice the Law of Action: taking action, so you get a reaction from the universe. This is a 50/50 job, and the universe WILL do its part — now, it's up to you to have the life-force energy to act.

4. **Trust:** Believe in the process and trust you are worthy of your desires. Trust that the path you're being led down will lead you exactly where you want to be. Trusting puts you in the high vibration of "belief," which keeps you on the right path. Know that your desire is already in your vortex and it will show up in perfect timing.

5. **Notice:** Pay attention to and celebrate the signs that are being sent your way. (For a refresher on signs, go back to day 16!) Give the universe credit when you're on your way and remember to say THANK YOU! And have fun on your journey! That's what this is about! Look for the gifts in the moment whenever possible, rather than focusing on what's not here yet.

Elevate The Globe's 7 Manifesting Steps

6. **High vibes:** Keep your vibration high so you aren't spiraling down into the lower vibration of "wanting" and you're continuing to become a match for what you are manifesting. This is where our daily Kundalini practice comes in. Having a morning ritual is a great way of connecting to your truth and the highest vibrations available to you every day so that you're attracting from that place.

7. **Release:** Let go, relax, and have fun! Know that everything you're manifesting is on its way in the most divine form. Don't keep asking — just enjoy and celebrate the path to getting there. This doesn't mean forgetting about what you asked for, it just means releasing control of how you think your desire will be delivered to you. It may show up differently than you expected. (And probably even better.)

Manifesting gets to be easy and quick once you know you're deserving of anything and everything you want. Your desires and dreams are yours for a reason. It's about dreaming BIG and looking past what you thought was possible or what you think your life can be. Look at what YOU really want. How do YOU want to feel? Anything that isn't aligned with that truth is a NO!

TODAY'S CHALLENGE

We're going to send some major energy towards at least one thing you want to manifest. If you're new to manifesting, start with something small to build your belief. Or if you've done this before, choose something REALLY big!

Write it down here.

_____

_____

_____

_____

Then, sit in silence and ask the universe for it.

Take a minute to feel it with all of your senses. Visualize what this would mean in your life and what it would look like manifested. Who is this version of you that receives and lives in the energy of your manifestation? Feel it, see it, enjoy it!

Write down at least one action you can take in the near future to move along this manifestation. If you don't know what that would look like, ask to be shown. Once you think of something, write it here and when you are going to do it. Add any details involved.

First Inspired Action: _____

Additional Action Items: _____

_____

_____

_____

_____

Now, all you have to do is work on your mindset around trusting, notice how things are coming together, keep your vibes high with the tools in this challenge, and RELEASE IT. Don't obsess over your manifestation — just be cool. Stay relaxed, keep taking action when you receive the inspiration, and have fun!

Keep us posted on what you're manifesting in the **Elevate The Globe Spiritual Warriors** Facebook group. And feel free to repeat this process with everything you want to manifest.

Bonus Challenge: Create a digital or physical vision board. We like to do ours in our journals. A lot of 528 Academy members create a digital vision board that they set as their desktop or phone screensaver, or you can create a board on Pinterest. Just pull some pictures together and put it somewhere you can see it. It can be simple — just one image to start is excellent. We would love to see these, so tag us on Instagram (@elevatetheglobe) or post in the Facebook group!

Ok, we have one more awesome day tomorrow. We are cheering you on and so excited for you to GO BIG with Day 21. See you there!!

DAY 21: Send Love to Your Mother (Earth)

You guys! We're on day 21! Elevating higher with you has been such a fun and amazing ride. We're about to get into some serious celebrating, but we couldn't complete this challenge without giving a little more love to Mother Earth first. She is our HOME, and she deserves just as much love and respect as our own domestic homes.

As we become aware of our own inner being and the subtle energy that's always around us, we gain a higher perspective. We can see how poorly Mother Earth is being treated, how much pain and anger from within her is coming out to be released. We see this in global warming and the form of natural disasters — like volcano eruptions, earthquakes, landslides, and floods — and in school shootings and international conflicts, in racism and hate. Then on the other side, because we live on a polarity planet, we see all of the positive ways people are creating change towards a better world.

As we've learned, everything is energy. The more positive, loving, caring, compassionate energy we give to Mother Earth, the more of the same energy we'll get back in return from her. (Because like attracts like, remember?)

To do this, we must start to pay attention, to increase our awareness of how we're currently treating the environment, and then vow to be a HUGE positive part of the solution. We must first start to notice our current habits, and from there we can begin to adjust our habits to create positive shifts.

TODAY'S CHALLENGE

Write down every single item that you use in one day, from your coffee mug and your to-go lunch container to your phone and your car.

Make your list here:

_____   _____

_____   _____

_____   _____

_____   _____

_____   _____

_____   _____

_____   _____

_____   _____

At the end of the day, witness how much you consumed. Begin to think about how everything you used today was created — from a conscious, sustainable place, or not? And if you threw anything away, do you know where it's going and what's going to become of it?

Scan your list for ways you can cut down on your consumption. Can you replace your to-go coffee cup with a reusable mug? Can you travel with a reusable fork, knife & spoon? What can you do to reduce how much you consume each day?

You've completed the 21-Day Elevate Higher Challenge!

It's time to celebrate and really look at how far you've come! Think about it: In just 21 days, you've added meditation, breathwork, and Kundalini yoga to your daily routine. You've cleaned up your social circle, your home, your finances, your environmental footprint, and your grocery list. You got to know yourself better through astrology and numerology, and you took time out for self-care. Oh, and you took the first concrete steps towards manifesting your wildest dreams — that's a HUGE deal.

Give yourself props right now, because celebrating is a form of gratitude for yourself and your accomplishments. Like we mentioned before, it's vital to be grateful for this exact time and space in your evolutionary journey if you want to keep moving forward.

We are so insanely happy for you and excited to see where the rest of your journey takes you. Keep using your favorite tools from this challenge to elevate yourself on a daily basis. We love you and are here for you, and we can't wait to work with you more and witness how this entire community continues to ELEVATE HIGHER!!!

Cue the confetti ...

Okay, so there's one last and final piece for you to tie a HUGE bow on this whole journey and come full circle.

TODAY'S CHALLENGE

Look back at the pre-challenge prep work and see how you felt before you started. Make a list of what's changed since then. How have you grown, and how does it feel to have committed and finished this work?

Journal about how you're feeling, how you've evolved, anything this journey has sparked within you, and what you've manifested so far. It could be a simple shift in mindset or a big thing you've released or brought into your life since the challenge started!

If you find yourself thinking of how far you still have to go, try to keep a positive mindset and really find gratitude for how far you've come. Revel in the miraculous journey you're on and celebrate being alive. Give yourself a ton of love and appreciation for all of the energy you put into this challenge and do something fun to honor YOU!

Oh, and keep in touch! Whether this is the first time you've worked with us or the hundredth, we hope to continue to connect with you and guide you in any way we can. We really can't EXPLAIN the love we have for you. We are so excited to see what incredible things come out of this challenge and how you continue to become more you, influence those around you, and help our community make massive change and elevate the globe!

Thank you for being you and for showing up.

nothing but love,

Britt + Tara

Sources

Pages 16-17. 3HO.com

Page 32. https://www.spiritvoyage.com

Page 48. https://www.nationalgeographic.com/magazine/2018/08/embark-essay-aggression-internet-twitter-human-nature/h

Page 51. https://www.3ho.org/3ho-lifestyle/5-sutras-aquarian-age/1st-sutra-recognize-other-person-you/recognize-other-person-you

Page 58. https://www.3ho.org/kundalini-yoga/mantra/kundalini-yoga-mantras/yogic-living-mantra-toolkit

Page 63. https://www.ewg.org/skindeep/why-this-matters-cosmetics-and-your-health/
https://www.sciencedaily.com/releases/2015/10/151023084508.htm
https://www.ewg.org/skindeep/
https://www.ewg.org/guides/cleaners

Page 73. https://www.prolificliving.com/money-affirmations/

Page 79. http://www.naturalawakeningssa.com/super-charged-high-and-low-frequencies-in-foods-in-our-bodies/

Page 82. Questions from Food as Medicine by Dharma Singh Khalsa, MD

Page 98. https://www.happify.com/hd/the-science-behind-gratitude/
http://greatergood.berkeley.edu/article/item/why_gratitude_is_good/

Page 100. https://soulpancake.com/portfolio_page/science-of-happiness/

Printed in Great Britain
by Amazon